For the ones who still have questions—
this isn't judgment. It's a spiritual investigation.
— Stevie Prince

WHERE WAS GOD?

The Charlie Kirk Connection

WillHouse

WHERE WAS GOD?

Published by WillHouse Media Group LLC

Cover design © WillHouse Media Group LLC

Interior design © WillHouse Media Group LLC

ISBN 979-8-9938756-0-6 (Paperback)

ISBN 979-8-9938756-1-3 (Hardcover)

Printed in the United States of America

Contents

DISCLAIMER & INVITATION

This book invites you into a spiritual and cultural investigation—one shaped by publicly available events, interviews, statements, and moments in history that have echoed across generations.

Every reference in these pages is drawn from the public record. Nothing here claims to reveal private motives or unseen intentions. What follows is commentary, interpretation, and reflection—an honest attempt to understand patterns, themes, and questions that have stirred in the hearts of many.

No individual, family, organization, or public figure mentioned in this work has participated in its creation, endorsed its conclusions, or contributed to its content. Their lives and words appear only in connection with material already in the public domain.

This investigation is offered with humility and reverence—not to judge, but to observe; not to condemn, but to discern; not to assign blame, but to explore the spiritual implications woven throughout the stories that shape our culture.

As you enter these pages, consider this your invitation: not into a verdict, but into a journey.

AUTHOR'S NOTE

The lights were still flashing when the questions began.

Headlines turned into hashtags. Faith turned into fallout.

And somewhere between the noise and the silence, one question refused to die:

Where was God?

This spiritual investigation will challenge everything you think you know about spiritual warfare, prayer, authority, and history— and may even reveal the possibility that God Himself was framed for a crime He never committed.

This book is bigger than one man.

It isn't a political statement. It isn't a fight between Catholics and Protestants. It's a spiritual investigation.

From the very beginning, I knew this story—though it touches names, dates, and tragedy—could never be about sides or labels. Whether you're a fan or a critic of Charlie Kirk, a lifelong believer or someone still deciding what you believe, this book was written for you.

Every claim, every connection, and every reference inside these pages was researched carefully and prayerfully. Every claim and reference in this book is based solely on publicly available statements, interviews, and records. We verified each detail carefully and approached every individual mentioned with humility and respect, without assuming motives or speaking beyond what is already public. For clarity, no individual or organization mentioned in these pages has reviewed, approved, contributed to, endorsed, or is associated with this book in any way; all references are drawn entirely from the public record. See the bibliography for citations.

Still, every word that remains was written with humility and reverence—to honor the legacy of Charlie Kirk, his family, and every person mentioned in these pages; to comfort those left behind; and to awaken the Church to questions far greater than denomination or dogma. This is not a book designed to divide, but to discern.

It's for the seeker searching for truth.

It's for the skeptic who's almost ready to believe.

It's for the theologian who still wonders where mystery ends and revelation begins.

This investigation started long before I ever heard the name Charlie Kirk. But when tragedy struck—when the news broke that he had been shot—it became the catalyst that finished what had already begun.

I didn't want to write this book. I wrestled with it. I delayed it. I even tried to bury it.

But after months of prayer, study, and sleepless conviction, I realized obedience sometimes sounds like a whisper that won't go away.

And if I'm being honest, this moment started long before these pages. More than thirteen years ago, when I found myself deep in a dark hole—living a double life as a pastor's kid, convinced God had written me off—I made a pact with Him. I told Him that if He ever pulled me out of that pit, I would spend the rest of my life telling the world that He still rescues people as dirty and as lost as I was.

So what follows next isn't just a book. It's a promise kept.
It's me doing what I told God I would do.

In the photo gallery, you'll see a picture of me holding a book, a bottle of Fanta in front of me, and a pack of chocolate turtles beside it. That photo was taken thirteen years ago—right after I hit rock bottom, slowly trying to find my faith again.

I had just experienced one of the most humiliating moments of my life. One of my mentors had let me stay in his trailer in South Florida—a place to reset while I picked up the pieces and figured out my next step. That trailer sat on the property behind a small Christian library.

I remember walking down the street to a Wendy's and getting rejected when I couldn't scrape together enough change to buy a chicken sandwich. I had spent some of my last dollars the day before on the book you see in that photo. It felt like a foolish purchase at the time, but God used it to start something I couldn't see yet.

He's brought me a long way since then.

And there's a reason I end this story—this investigation—on Chapter 13.

Because the same grace that found me in that trailer park is the grace that wrote this book.

What comes next…is that story.

So get ready.

Buckle up.

The case file has been opened.

Let's find out where God was when we needed Him the most.

PROLOGUE

The Clarification

It happened the first week of November 2025.

Just days before this book went to print, an extraordinary shift rippled through the Christian world. A newly appointed pope, Pope Leo XIV, approved a decree called *Mater Populi Fidelis*—"The Mother of the Faithful People of God."

The document instructed Catholics to stop using the titles "*co-redeemer*" or "*co-redemptrix*" for Mary. The Vatican clarified that while Mary's role in giving birth to Jesus was essential, it was a subordinate role—and that only Jesus saved humanity through His death on the cross.

Whatever the pope's intention, it's a good thing that even now, more than a billion souls are being pointed straight back to Jesus Christ—the Man with the beard I met in that sketchy hotel room…the One who gave me restful sleep when my soul was a storm.

Overnight, one of the oldest religious institutions on Earth found itself thrust into the headlines, sparking confusion, relief, anger, and reflection in equal measure.

Across social media, Catholic believers wrestled with disbelief. Some felt betrayed, wondering how a man could, with the stroke of a pen, alter a belief system their grandparents lived and died with. Evangelical Christians, on the other hand, pointed fingers—some gloating, others grieving—asking, "If they were wrong about something this big, what else might be built on sand?"

But let me be clear—this isn't a political book.

It isn't written to pit Catholics against Protestants or anyone against anyone.

This is a spiritual investigation—a search for patterns that stretch from the Garden of Eden to modern stages and statehouses, from thrones to tour buses, from royalty to presidents, pop stars, and ordinary people alike.

It's a story much bigger than one man, one movement, or one denomination.

Because in heaven, there won't be a Catholic section or a Protestant section.

There will be one table.

One massive celebration.

One family.

Open your heart.
And let the investigation begin.

THE EVIDENCE BOARD

1

WHY DOES GOD ALLOW EVIL?

The Freedom Paradox

Love's greatest gift became evil's favorite weapon.

My doorbell rang.

A FedEx driver left a small white box on the porch—nothing special at first glance. But I knew exactly what it was. Evidence.

Inside, folded tight, lay a white T-shirt—seven bold letters printed across the front:

FREEDOM

In the weeks after Charlie's assassination, the internet lit up with people selling that shirt—some out of support, some out of exploitation. I wasn't trying to get wrapped up in the conspiracy theories. I was thinking about clues.

I carried it to my office, where a wall of corkboard had turned into a collage of questions: newspaper clippings, Scriptures, quotes, timelines—red string pulling them together like arteries. I pinned the shirt to the center.

Then I sat back in my chair and stared.

How could a word that sounds liberating end up tagged as evidence at a crime scene?

Charlie loved this country. From the looks of it, freedom was one of his favorite words. As those seven letters stared back at me from the wall, I couldn't shake the weight of it.

America was closing in on her 250th anniversary—the land of the free, the home of the brave. Two-and-a-half centuries of a nation built on liberty. Yet somehow, the word that defined her ended up pinned to my evidence board like a crime scene clue.

From the Grand Canyon to Hollywood, from Nashville's backroads to Chicago's skyline, freedom has always been America's siren song—strong enough to make people cross oceans, deserts, and even shark-infested waters just to touch the promise.

Freedom.

I remember a clip where Charlie explained that if people could engage in civil discourse—understand the First Amendment, the freedom of speech, the idea of limited government—then maybe, just maybe, they'd follow that string back to the original Architect of freedom.

And then I asked the question I'd been avoiding:

How could God allow evil to do this?

As I thought of the word *evil*, an image flashed across my mind.

A *tree*.

I was sure I'd heard it before: a tree of good and evil. I rushed to open the Scriptures and found myself back in Genesis—the story of creation, intelligent design, a story that pivots around a tree.

We've all heard the Sunday school version. Even if you don't believe in God, you've heard the narrative: a garden called Eden, the first humans, a woman named Eve reaching for forbidden fruit. Painters made it an apple. I don't think it was an apple—but that's not the point.

The point was the tree.

I put my investigator hat back on.

What if the tree wasn't primarily a test? Not a cruel trick placed by a God waiting for humans to fail. What if the tree was a mirror—showing humanity what it becomes when it tries to define morality without its Maker?

I sat with that for days.

The thought followed me everywhere—into the shower, into traffic, into the silence before sleep.

Every time I tried to move on, it whispered back:

What if the tree was a mirror?

Then my doorbell rang again.

Another package.

IKEA—the massive Swedish furniture company known for its flat boxes and "some assembly required" chaos.

I needed to set up a desk and a bookshelf in another room. And as if God Himself was winking at me, the boxes were heavy with the other American epidemic: the freedom to ignore instructions.

I'm not the only one who's been elbow-deep in cardboard, expecting a desk and finding a thousand pieces, an Allen wrench shaped like a question mark, and three mystery screws that never find a home. It took me back to childhood—my father dragging a box in from the furniture store, waving off the instructions like he was swatting a fly, telling me to hand him his favorite cordless drill and "a few extra screws." He could see the final product in his mind, so he forced the parts to obey the picture in his head. It worked—kind of. The drawers stuck, the legs wobbled, the top leaned a degree or two to the left. But it stood.

Maybe I inherited that gene—the I-can-do-it-my-way gene.

By the time I was halfway through tightening bolts, my hands were fighting the furniture, and my mind was fighting something else. Somewhere between the crooked shelves and the missing screws, I couldn't stop thinking about that word again—freedom.

It felt almost orchestrated, like heaven was staging a metaphor right in my living room.

I reached for the Allen wrench in my left hand, then the instruction manual I'd been ignoring. And that's when I saw it—printed in red at the top of the page:

WARNING: *Risk of damage or injury. Follow all instructions. Do not misuse product.*

The kind of label meant to keep you from getting hurt or from using something outside its intended purpose.

I froze. The wrench slipped from my fingers.

I dropped the manual and walked straight to my evidence wall. No hesitation. I pinned another clue to the board—because suddenly it all connected.

Because it hit me. Long before IKEA—or any modern manufacturer—the God who created the heavens and the earth was the *first Manufacturer,* the *original Designer,* assembling creation with precision and intention.

And maybe that tree in the garden was His first warning label.
Then the clues began to click. The sweater started to unravel.
I found it.
Ancient words, glowing under a thousand years of dust:
"And the Lord God commanded the man, saying, Of every tree of the garden thou mayest freely eat: But of the tree of the knowledge of good and evil, thou shalt not eat of it: for in the day that thou eatest thereof thou shalt surely die."
—Genesis 2:16–17 (KJV)
Pause.

Remember the IKEA furniture? The instructions I refused to read? The desk that still slants?

Could it be that God, as the original Creator, placed His own warning label in Eden—the spiritual equivalent of the red tag on a hairdryer:

DANGER: *Risk of death. Do not use near water.*

We all follow that label. You don't step into the tub with a hairdryer. Not because you're a slave to the manufacturer, but because the one who made it knows what it can do—for good and for harm.

But spiritually? Humanity plugged in beside the bathtub. The shock hit the water and rippled across the centuries.

So why would God plant that tree at all?

That question is the paradox—

the Freedom Paradox.

Paradox (n.) — a truth so profound it appears to contradict itself until you see from a higher vantage.

Like the idea that strength is born in weakness. Or that freedom, to be real, must include the option to rebel.

If God is all-knowing, all-present, all-powerful—He had to have known what would happen.

So why plant the tree? Why risk it?

Because love without choice isn't love—it's programming.

All evidence points to a God who didn't want indentured servants…but a family.

Freedom is the risk love is willing to take.

I kept digging, hot on the trail.

The deeper I searched, the more the pattern repeated—freedom and risk, love and loss, choice and consequence. Every clue led me back to the same haunting question.

Then another verse surfaced—buried near the end of the Book—and it hit me like evidence hiding in plain sight:

"The Lamb slain from the foundation of the world."
—Revelation 13:8 (KJV)

Could it be that before He ever walked through the garden, He had already accepted the Cross?

Could it be that before He planted the tree, He knew His creation would one day nail Him **to a tree**?

The paradox deepened. The Architect of freedom had written grace into the blueprint before the first sin, before the first heartbeat.

He planted the tree—knowing the same breath He gave humanity would one day **shout**, "Crucify him!"

No anesthesia. No Tylenol. Pure pain…and a plan older than Eden.

I shouted out loud in my empty room—half in disbelief, "Why would God do this!?"

It didn't make sense! Not yet…

But something told me the answer was hidden inside that same word—*freedom.*

But as I read the creation story again, I realized God gave humans free will—the freedom to choose. He wasn't surprised when Adam and Eve betrayed Him. He wasn't shocked when they treated the manual like scrap paper, defined morality without the Giver of life, and aligned themselves with the serpent's script. He had written a rescue into the blueprint before page one.

Maybe you get that. Maybe you've messed up so profoundly you believed you surprised God—like your sin jumped out of a closet He didn't check. I told myself those lies. You'll see in the next chapter what happened when I finally confronted evil face-to-face. But even then, feeling disqualified, I was learning God was never surprised by my failures. He knew—and He still chose to die for me.

Sleep left me. I was up till almost three each morning, up again at six to take my child to school. Work by day, investigation by night— Scripture, headlines, history, prayer, and the strange quiet that falls when God starts rearranging furniture in your soul.

Yet something still didn't make sense—until a memory surfaced.

The last time I preached was more than ten years ago. I used to speak. I traveled. Big stages. Big names. I was a pastor's son—living a divided life. Things happened; people happened. I grew indifferent with God because of what people did to me. I blamed Him for their choices and, eventually, I walked away.

But I remembered the title of one message: "Who's Your Daddy?"

I pulled up the old footage. I watched a younger me talking about Jesus at Easter time because that's what everyone does at Easter time— even a man who didn't fully understand what he was preaching. I had found something peculiar then and it struck me again now. After the resurrection, the first person Jesus meets is Mary. She recognizes Him outside the empty tomb, and as she moves toward Him—maybe to hug Him—He says something I've never gotten over:

"Jesus saith unto her, Touch me not; for I am not yet ascended to my Father: but go to my brethren, and say unto them, I ascend unto my Father, and your Father; and to my God, and your God." —John 20:17 KJV

He didn't step out of the grave with a crown on His head and a set of demands saying: "Bow to your Master."

No—He came out speaking family.

"My Father and your Father."

Even in victory, He was revealing the first thing about God's heart: Father.

And for a man like me, starved for a deeper relationship with my dad, that landed where nothing else could.

Still, life spun. I drifted. And for years the same burning question haunted me:

Where was God?

One day, staring at the evidence wall, the answer leapt at me like a wave:

We nailed Him to a tree. That's where He was.

In the mud.

Eating with sinners (they called Him the friend of publicans and sinners).

Loving the family He wanted from the start. Not algorithms. Not code. Humans—with the freedom to stay or walk away.

Everything circled back to those seven letters dangling from a pushpin.

It all reduces to the scandalous paradox: Freedom.

And then the verbs began to echo—two phrases, thousands of years apart, vibrating across Scripture like a tuning fork.

Eve: "She took…and did eat" (Genesis 3:6 KJV).

Jesus: "Take, eat; this is my body" (Matthew 26:26 KJV).

Same verbs. Same humanity. Different outcome.

The first tree cracked eternity open with death and evil.

The second opened it with life.

The first tree ushered in sin and death.

The second—Calvary—offered salvation and adoption into the family business.

Freedom is powerful—and dangerous. In the hands of love, it liberates captives. In the hands of malice, it justifies atrocities: innocent lives taken, senseless wars, families splintered. We call all of it evil.

Let's zoom in on that word.

The Hebrew term for *evil* in Genesis is עַר (ra'). Joseph—the dreamer with the coat of many colors—used that same word when he | 25 finally faced the brothers who'd betrayed him, thrown him into a pit, and sold him into slavery. After God flipped the script and set Joseph in Pharaoh's palace, he told them:

"But as for you, ye thought evil against me; but God meant it unto good." —Genesis 50:20 KJV

The original Hebrew reads: "You planned evil" (עַר סְתְבְּשָׁח, chashavtem ra'); "God re-planned it for good" (הַבּוֹטל הָבָשָׁח, chashavah le-tovah).

Same object. Different planner. A divine reweaving, not a divine conspiracy.

God didn't author the evil. He flipped it.

Later, when Jesus taught His disciples to pray, the language intensifies:

> "And lead us not into temptation, but deliver us from evil: For thine is the kingdom, and the power, and the glory, for ever. Amen." —Matthew 6:13 KJV

The original Greek reads: τοῦ πονηροῦ (tou ponērou)—not merely moral wrongdoing but a malignant personality: the evil one.

So:

Old Testament evil = what man does.

New Testament evil = who opposes God.

In both? It didn't come from God. It's what He came to destroy.

It's ironic that Michael Jackson sang about the man in the mirror. That concept is older than any chart. Since Eden, humanity has been staring into a mirror—one tree reflecting rebellion; another reflecting redemption.

And long before Cain raised his hand against Abel, the first crime scene was a garden. The first con job. The first scam. The same Satan who misused his free will and tried to usurp God left fingerprints in Eden—seducing, twisting, coaxing humans to ignore the warning label. He couldn't wound God directly, so he targeted the image of God—us.

God gave a warning in the garden—a label that could have been printed in red:

DANGER: RISK OF DEATH IF YOU USE FREEDOM INCORRECTLY.

Not because He was afraid. Not because He wanted to control. Because He knew what we were capable of—what we would choose— and still refused to remove our agency. That's not weakness.

That's freedom.

The apostles wrote about it too. We throw the word around, but Scripture puts a stake in the ground:

> "For ye have not received the spirit of *bondage* again to fear; but ye have received the Spirit of adoption, whereby we cry, Abba, Father." —Romans 8:15 KJV

And it came to me: What's the antithesis of bondage?

FREEDOM.
Freedom from fear. Freedom from sin. Freedom from your past. Freedom from the evil one.

Love's greatest gift = FREEDOM

became EVIL's favorite weapon.

I pinned another note beside the shirt and said the line out loud— the one that would carry me into the next case file: Me.
That's when it got wild…
I realized—I was haunted.

2

THE SHOT
HEARD AROUND
THE WORLD

Reopening Heaven's Oldest Cold Case

It started because something didn't sit right...

It was one of those almost-too-perfect days in September—the kind where the sun lingers a little longer in the sky, as if even heaven wanted to savor the warmth before fall arrived. I was sitting in the bleachers of a gymnastics meet for one of my daughters, clapping politely with the other parents, taking little videos, proud of the small victories only parents understand. Children's laughter echoed against the rafters. For a moment, everything was ordinary.

Then my phone buzzed.

"Charlie Kirk is dead."

My stomach dropped. The air seemed to vanish from the room—as if someone had punched a hole through the universe and the oxygen fled.

Another message came through:

"No wait…scratch that. He's stable."

Then, minutes later:
"Confirmed. He's dead."

For those who may not know the name, Charlie Kirk was a political commentator and the founder of Turning Point USA—one of the largest youth organizations for political engagement in America. He was also an outspoken evangelical Christian whose boldness and unapologetic defense of faith made him both admired and attacked.

But this book isn't a Charlie Kirk biography.

It's not about politics or parties.

It's about patterns—spiritual ones.

And that matters, because what happened to Charlie wasn't just a headline or a tragedy. It was the opening line of an investigation that stretches far beyond one man, one moment, or even one movement—into questions that reach all of us.

I stared at my phone, blinking, as the world kept spinning around me—cartwheels on the mat, applause in the stands, while something inside me went still. Not because I was a mega-fan. Not because I followed Charlie's every move. But because I knew who he was. And, more importantly, what he stood for: boldness, family, conviction in a culture that rewards compromise.

No matter your politics, if you have even a drop of respect for courage, Charlie Kirk was someone to watch.

He didn't hide behind a camera.

He walked into hostile rooms.

He debated live, without teleprompters.

And he did it unafraid.

That's rare.

That's admirable.

And then suddenly—like a scene that doesn't belong in the movie—he was gone.

I didn't know him personally. But that day, it felt personal. And to be honest with you, I'd felt that feeling before—the gut punch. The sudden silence after an important voice is taken from the world.

Go back with me ten years. Location: Miami. Sun blazing. The stadium packed. And on stage was Dr. Myles Munroe, a global faith leader, best-selling author, and trusted advisor to presidents and business leaders alike. He wasn't flashy. He wasn't trying to build a brand. He was building people. His messages on purpose, identity, and kingdom leadership had transformed lives from Wall Street to third-world villages.

He spoke with such weight, such fire, it felt like the words weren't just coming from a man—but through him. He didn't shout. He declared. And when you heard him speak, it was like hearing someone who had been in the throne room of heaven and brought back notes.

Months after that event, his plane crashed.

Gone.

With his wife.

With his team.

I remember exactly where I was. I remember not believing it. Because people like that aren't supposed to die like that.

Not mid-mission.

Not with so much more to do.

And certainly not that way.

Years later, old clips surfaced online—Myles himself, preaching, joking about how much he loved his wife, saying his plan was to die with her. In another sermon, he referenced, almost hypothetically, what it would mean if someone like him died in a plane crash. It chilled me.

Could a man so full of purpose have accidentally spoken a sentence that echoed forward?

Could words, even casual ones, open unseen doors?

Those questions lingered. They burned.

And when I later heard the news about Charlie, it was as if those same questions came knocking again.

Now pause.

You don't have to be a Christian to read this book. You don't have to be a person of faith—you might be a seeker, a skeptic, a fan, or a critic.

What began to unravel was much bigger than one man. To understand why I couldn't let this go, you need a little context about me. I grew up around music—records stacked like bricks of memory. My parents met in a band. My father was the drummer for a Spanish group that dressed like the Beatles—cummerbunds, bow ties, polished shoes. My mother was their lead singer. Rhythm and harmony were my inheritance.

Some kids grew up on playgrounds; I grew up in rehearsals. Friday nights meant folding chairs at band practice, told to stay still while trombones tuned and guitars hummed. There were no iPads back then—just imagination. My G.I. Joe action figure became a soldier on missions across the carpet; a sneaker turned into a tank; my Pee-wee Herman toy was my sidekick. Since there were no video games to disappear into, I had to build worlds in my head.

In those band rehearsals, I learned to watch—to feel the beat, to see harmony and chord patterns before I ever played a note. Later, that closeness to music opened unexpected doors. As a young producer, my first entertainment attorney connected me to the Chicago Chapter of the Recording Academy, the organization behind the Grammys. I became one of its youngest nomination-review committee members, sworn to secrecy, flown from Chicago to Santa Monica to deliberate with the biggest names in music.

I remember the long table overlooking the Santa Monica Pier—name cards from MTV, record labels, and producers I'd only ever seen in liner notes. The room had a quiet electricity to it. No cameras. No fans. Just coffee cups, ballots, and reputations on the line. Behind those doors, we weren't there to chase trends—we were the gatekeepers, deciding what counted as the best in the world's biggest music award show.

"You'll only hear the first twenty seconds of each track."

Twenty seconds—that was all we had to judge a song's soul. No choruses. No bridges. Just a flash of melody, lyric, tone, and production before the next file loaded.

The playlist rolled like a conveyor belt of greatness—legends, newcomers, even Beyoncé.

We scribbled notes under the weight of it all, knowing one small checkmark could shift a career forever.

It was thrilling. Intimidating. Surreal for a dreamer kid from Northwest Indiana.

Those experiences stretched me. They taught me that art, faith, and darkness often share the same stage. That's why, when I hear headlines that sound like destiny collapsing, I don't just feel them—I investigate them.

I loved history as much as harmony. I remember learning about Lincoln's assassination, Reagan's attempted, and Elvis's death—assuming they were random tragedies. Later, I toured Graceland and felt the tension between fame and fragility. The mix of brilliance and brokenness fascinated me. Little did I know that same curiosity would become crucial when it came to writing this book.

This isn't a political project.

It's an investigation.

Fast-forward a decade, and I'm back in the bleachers, phone in hand, reading headlines about Charlie Kirk being gunned down—live, on camera, in front of thousands.

They called it a debate.

But it ended in execution.

That video—the one I wish I had never opened—has been watched by millions. But for me, it isn't *viral*.

It's visceral.

Charlie sits there—confident, alert, ready to engage ideas with ideas.

Then the shot.

Then the scream.

Then the world froze.

That's the moment I felt something crack inside me again, not just sadness, but that old spiritual disorientation that comes when the good guys get taken out. Because it wasn't just Charlie. There was a deeper connection to my past. It felt like déjà vu. And each time it happened—whether with Myles Munroe or other well-known voices—the same question rose in my soul:

Where was God?

After the shot, Charlie's body was rushed behind the podium and into a black SUV. From there, the chaos only intensified. Eyewitnesses say his team screamed for help, tried to stop the bleeding, and began CPR. Horns blared as they weaved through traffic toward the nearest hospital.

I wasn't in that SUV. But I imagine every second felt like eternity—stretched between urgency, hope, and horror. I honor those who did their best with what they knew—fighting to keep Charlie alive amid the chaos.

Aside from the assassin, I couldn't shake the sense that something darker was hiding behind the trigger. Something that didn't bleed—but moved things that did. And like many of you, I asked the question that haunts every tragedy:

Why would a loving God allow evil to exist?

For weeks, I couldn't sleep. I prayed for clarity, for wisdom, for the truth behind what had happened. The truth is—this whole project began as therapy.

Not in response to the noise.

Not for clicks or clout.

| 35

No. It was deeper than that.

It was spiritual.

It started as something personal, a way to wrestle with what I was seeing and sensing. A kind of self-ministry, a private attempt to dig for truth. And somewhere along the way, it became a manuscript.

As I dug through history, connecting dots between other lives cut short, I began to see that same villain's fingerprints everywhere.

Different faces.

Different decades.

Different victims.

Same darkness.

I'm a man of faith, not perfect, but persistent. I believe in angels. I believe in Psalm 91—a passage many consider one of the most powerful in all of Scripture, declaring God's protection over those who trust Him: "A thousand may fall at your side, ten thousand at your right hand, but it will not come near you." (v. 7 NIV).

But that day, it did.

Again.

To someone who, by all appearances, was walking in purpose and boldness.

So if I'm honest, this book didn't start because I wanted to write it. It started because something kept tugging—quietly, relentlessly—like a thread I couldn't ignore. It started because something didn't sit right. And maybe you've felt it too—that tension between what we claim to believe and what keeps happening to the people we admire most.

In the days after Charlie's death, unspoken questions surfaced everywhere—message boards, DMs, late-night podcasts. But few dared to challenge the narrative. Instead, we heard:

"God needed him in heaven."

"He paid the ultimate price."

"He was a martyr for truth."

"His death will bring revival."

All that sounds noble. But deep down, I kept thinking—he should have lived.

Let me say this clearly: I honor Charlie Kirk—his family, his legacy, his courage.

This isn't an attack or a political rant. It's my attempt to process the gut punch of not just what happened—but what didn't happen. And to ask, like a man standing at a crime scene:

Did the Church go silent?

Did we confuse tragedy with testimony?

Did we start calling early death holy just to make sense of our own powerlessness?

Because something tells me this wasn't just a moment. It was a message.

Why do so many lives—faithful or faithless, voices of light and voices still searching—end so tragically?

Shot.
Crashed.

Collapsed.

Slandered into silence.

Removed without warning.

And every time, the narrative is polished:

"God called them home."

"His race was finished."

"He died a martyr."

But here's what we don't say:

They were targeted—spiritually targeted.

And when I searched through history's case files, I saw the same pattern repeating.

No one condemned.

No one declared life.

No one challenged the curse. | 37

This book will.

Because in the hours after Charlie's death, whispers surfaced—witches bragging on Etsy and Reddit about spell-casting, hexes, rituals done to silence him.

Some say they were paid.

Some say it's a hoax.

But what no one said was:

What if it wasn't?

And what if we never resisted it?

In the days after, videos spiraled. Conspiracy theories from every corner. Within hours, people were already fighting over Charlie's legacy. Some influencers rushed same-day videos claiming they knew the "real Charlie Kirk." Others debated whether he had shifted faith— still Protestant, Evangelical, or newly Catholic?

I was in shock—not because this was happening months later, but within minutes.

Then something else surfaced.

Megyn Kelly, a trusted voice and close friend of the Kirks, released a video confirming what many had only whispered. According to Kelly—speaking from her conversation with Erika Kirk—the couple had read the disturbing magazine article in *Jezebel* just two days before the shooting. The article bragged about hiring witches on Etsy— multiple witches—to place curses on Charlie Kirk. And according to Kelly, Charlie and Erika were "rattled." So afraid that the night before the shooting they called a priest, a close family friend, to pray over Charlie.

The next day, he was murdered.

That was the moment my journal became a manuscript—the moment I realized I couldn't keep this private anymore.

I had to write.

I had to dig.

I had to speak.

Am I saying that any magazine article—or a few witches online— had the power to murder anyone? No.

However, this investigation will reveal unsettling connections— premonitions spoken, phrases repeated, and patterns that almost sound like alignment with darkness.

Words are far more powerful than we think.

Am I saying those Etsy witches had more power than a Spirit-filled believer? Absolutely not.

But when lies are spoken and truth stays silent, there seems to be a spiritual law at work—one that doesn't play favorites.

And if we're honest with ourselves, it's *worth investigating*.

Not because we can change the past…

But because we might be able to change the future.

As I pieced details together, the timing grew eerie, the silence deafening, and the dots began to connect. What you're about to learn will shock you.

If you've ever lost someone too soon…

If you've watched a leader fall…

If you've felt the sting of silence after spiritual warfare…

Then this book is for you.

If you've wondered why we don't see divine intervention anymore…

If you've been confused by contradictions in protection theology…

If you've seen "no weapon formed against me" look like it failed…

Then this book is your mirror.

Because the shot heard around the world didn't just end a man's life—it opened a case file.

Not just on one man, or one movement—but on all of us.

These spiritual crime scenes have stirred questions that echo through history—about why the same patterns keep repeating, and who will finally connect the dots.

And as I sat in those bleachers, phone in hand, the laughter of children echoing, one question looped in my head like a song you can't stop humming:

Could this have been prevented?

Was there a connection—not just between Charlie Kirk and Myles Munroe, but between presidents, pop stars, prophets, and performers—all gone too soon? Was something more evil at play—something no one had yet connected?

That question wouldn't leave me.

It stalked me through the night, through scrolls and headlines, tugging at the thread until the whole sweater began to unravel. As I kept digging—re-watching interviews, re-reading obituaries—a pattern emerged across decades, nations, industries. A pattern that made my blood run cold.

What if this wasn't random?

What if this wasn't just politics?

What if the real story has never been told?

That's when I knew I couldn't stay silent. The evidence was stacking itself—not on a desk, but in my spirit.

What if the pattern wasn't random at all? What if the same force that whispered to prophets was whispering to presidents—turning premonitions into countdowns? Because the investigation reveals something chilling: they all said the same things before they tragically died. Bizarrely, they all acted in the same way. And whether it was a respected man of God or a rock star, each may have been their own closest prophet—unwittingly predicting the very fate they feared.

3

PREMONITION OR PERMISSION

A Witch in the White House

Was it a warning from Heaven—or an invitation from hell?

The sun was setting over Washington D.C., March 1863.

The Civil War was bleeding across the nation. Inside the White House, a different kind of war was stirring—one not fought with muskets but with spirits. Abraham Lincoln's young son Willie had died of typhoid the year before, and the loss had carved a hollow in the First Lady's heart that nothing on Earth could fill.

From the cobblestone streets outside, the clip-clop of horse hooves echoed against the winter air. A velvet-draped carriage slowed to a stop at the gates of 1600 Pennsylvania Avenue. Its brass lanterns flickered in the fog. The driver, gloved hands steady, face half-hidden beneath his hat pulled back a curtain. Inside sat a woman in black. Her eyes glimmered with something that was not quite grief and not quite peace. She had been summoned by name.

A White House guard stepped forward, lantern in hand. He opened the carriage door, the smell of wet leather, hay, and coal smoke curling into the night. The woman stepped down slowly, her skirt brushing the frozen mud. She wasn't a dignitary. She wasn't a foreign emissary. She was a medium—some called her a witch. And that night, she would be escorted to that famous room in the White House—known as the *Red Room*.

You might be wondering if this book just turned into fiction.

It didn't.

This scene isn't a movie script. It happened. Or at least, something very close to it.

As I began following the trail of evidence, every breadcrumb led me here—to the White House itself. On March 4, 1861, Abraham

Lincoln was sworn in as the sixteenth president of the United States. The country was breaking apart at the seams. But two years later, another fracture opened—not in the Union, but in the Lincoln home. February 20, 1862, their eleven-year-old son Willie died in the very halls of the White House. The grief was unbearable. It drove *Mary Todd Lincoln* into the arms of spiritualism.

By 1862 and 1863, séances were being held in that crimson-walled parlor known as the Red Room. *Spiritualism* itself was at its height. Across the nation, families torn apart by war and disease turned to *mediums*, believing they could speak once more to their dead sons and husbands. The line between grief and *necromancy* blurred. And what the Bible called forbidden—talking to the dead—was suddenly fashionable, even patriotic.

When I first read the story, I had to stop. It sounded like the opening scene of a Netflix horror documentary—fog, flickering candles, and a séance in the White House. But this wasn't Hollywood. It was history.

And even as I read it, I kept asking myself—where was God in all this? **How could the house built to lead a nation flirt with the spirits it was meant to resist.**

There are newspaper accounts like the *Boston Gazette*, 1863, reporting that President Lincoln himself permitted a correspondent to attend a *trance* sitting. The journalist described Lincoln in uncharacteristically good humor, joking with his aides while a *medium* allegedly *channeled* Henry Knox, George Washington's long-dead Secretary of War. Whether that story was exaggerated or not, the cultural mood of the moment was undeniable: *spiritualism* had made itself at home in the nation's house. The article was soon reprinted across the country, spreading whispers of the "*séances* in the Red Room."

Even Pulitzer Prize–winning biographer Carl Sandburg treated accounts like the *Boston Gazette* report with enough weight to include discussion of them in his Lincoln volumes.

Then came the dream.

Lincoln's friend and bodyguard, Ward Hill Lamon, later swore the president described it to him just days before the assassination— wandering the White House halls, hearing weeping, and finding a coffin guarded by soldiers. *"Who is dead in the White House?"* Lincoln had asked. The voice replied, *"The president. He was killed by an assassin."*

Days later, John Wilkes Booth pulled the trigger at Ford's Theatre.

Coincidence? Maybe. Maybe not.

Because what makes the story stranger still is this: records suggest Booth himself dabbled in the same *occult circles*, attending *séances* led by the very *mediums* once invited to the White House.

At that point, history stops feeling clean. It stops feeling safe.

You start to realize that behind the portraits and marble halls might have been something far older—something unseen.

Now, I'm not here to accuse or sensationalize. I'm simply following the evidence wherever it leads. Some theories about Lincoln border on myth, yes. But others—**documented**, **corroborated**, and **witnessed**—refuse to be ignored.

And oddly enough, the stories didn't end in the 1800s. They just changed voices.

Fast-forward a century and a half.

NBC's *Today Show*. One of **President George W. Bush's** twin daughters, Jenna Bush Hager, sits on the couch recounting her own night in the White House. She says she awoke to 1920s-style piano music coming through her fireplace. Opera, faint but unmistakable. It terrified her. She ran to her sister Barbara's room. Later, she told *Buddy Carter*, a White House staffer who had served ten presidents over nearly fifty years. His reply? *"Jenna, you wouldn't believe what I've heard."*

That line stopped me cold.

Because now the pattern stretched from Mary Todd Lincoln's | 45 *séances* in 1863 to Jenna Bush Hager's confession in the 2000s—and standing between them both, a butler who'd seen it all. *William "Buddy" Carter.* Forty-seven years of service. Trusted by presidents and first ladies from *Nixon* to *Biden*. Invited to weddings, funerals, and state dinners. So beloved that *President Trump* once delayed the Congressional Ball just to surprise him with a birthday cake in the State Floor ballroom.

If anyone knew the White House better than the presidents themselves, it was Buddy.

And even he admitted: you wouldn't believe what I've heard.
Maybe the ghosts of history don't stay quiet after all.

And maybe—just maybe—those echoes in the halls are trying to tell us something.

But what were they trying to say?

Was Lincoln's dream a heavenly warning—a merciful attempt from God to protect him?

Or was it something darker?

Was it *syncretism*, a dangerous mixture of faith and forbidden practice that opened the wrong door?

Had the president, perhaps unknowingly, invited the very forces that would later destroy him?

Or was grief itself the open door—a spiritual vulnerability that darkness knew how to exploit?

Was fear whispering the outcome before it happened—hoping he'd **speak it into existence?**

Or was the dream itself a kind of spiritual breach, a window cracked open by curiosity, grief, and sorrow?

These aren't comfortable questions.

But any serious investigator knows you don't ignore clues just because they make you uneasy.

I'm not writing this chapter to frighten anyone—or to disrespect the Lincolns. I'm writing it because sometimes *truth hides* in the tension between the seen and the unseen. Because maybe, just maybe, history isn't as tidy as we've been taught.

We like to think that if we close our eyes long enough, the darkness will stop existing.

That if we pretend there's nothing under the bed, there's nothing to fear.

But ignoring the spiritual realm doesn't erase it.

It only blinds us to what's really there.

So before we move forward, we have to ask:

Is the physical world all there is?

Or has the unseen been influencing the visible all along?

Because when the Commander-in-Chief dreams of his own death just days before it happens—

and the assassin himself sits in the same circles of spiritual darkness—

you can't just call that coincidence.

You have to investigate it.

Even if it makes you uncomfortable.

Let's dig deeper.

And yet Buddy Carter wasn't the only one to hear something in those halls.

President Harry S. Truman wrote to his wife in 1946:

> *"I jumped up and put on my bathrobe. Looked down the hall—no one. Locked the door and heard footsteps in your room. The damn place is haunted for sure."*

The Secret Service confirmed no one had been upstairs.

Decades later, **J.D. Vance**—by then Vice President of the United States—spent a night in the Lincoln Bedroom after President Trump showed him the desk where the Emancipation Proclamation was written.

Vance later admitted, *"It was the creepiest thing to sleep in that room."*

Over the years, others claimed to see him too—from Winston Churchill to Grace Coolidge, from visiting queens to staff who refused to enter the Lincoln Bedroom after dark. The details changed, but the description never did:

A tall, quiet figure—

watching,

waiting,

still walking the halls of power.

And yet…maybe that's precisely the point.

Why so many bizarre moments in a place meant for order and leadership?

Why so much paranormal whisper, fear, and dream?

It wasn't just history happening in those walls—something spiritual was unsettled there.

Because when a nation's leaders begin consulting mediums, hearing music in empty rooms, and dreaming of death, you have to ask the one question that won't leave you alone:

Where was God in all of it?

Even in the twenty-first century, the walls of 1600 Pennsylvania Avenue refused to stay silent.

Michelle Obama once told visiting children that she and **President Obama** heard strange noises in the hallway late at night—sounds even they couldn't explain (a detail reported by the Los Angeles Times and noted by the White House Historical Association).

That's not proof

But it's a *thread*.

A whisper from the present pulling you back into the past.

Could it all be just coincidence?

From presidents' children to queens and prime ministers, something supernatural—

or at least unexplainable—seems to linger in that house.

And even the **Reagan** era didn't escape the whispers.

Ronald and **Nancy** both spoke cautiously about *"odd things"* in the White House, but it was their children who said it out loud.

Michael Reagan admitted, *"I think there are ghosts in the White House…and I think my dad probably believed it too."*

His sister *Maureen* remembered staying overnight in the Lincoln Bedroom and waking to the smell of cigar smoke curling through the dark.

When she opened her door, she swore she saw a man in a stovepipe **hat standing near the fireplace.** *"I told Dad I'm never staying in that room again."*

Their little Cavalier King Charles spaniel, Rex, seemed to agree.

According to Michael, Rex would sometimes slip out of the presidential suite at night, trot down the hall, and stop outside the Lincoln Bedroom—barking furiously at the closed door, refusing to cross the threshold.

Reagan once tried to leash him and lead him inside.

The dog dug in, trembling, unmoving, "

for hell or high water."

Could it be that animals sense what we ignore—that even after a century of presidents, prayers, and renovations, something in that room still stirs when the lights go out?

But the story of the Reagans doesn't end with cigar smoke and a frightened dog.

It reaches deeper—into something eerily familiar.

Abraham Lincoln never formally joined a church. He often attended Presbyterian services with Mary, but when ministers pressed him for membership, he quietly declined.

His law partner called him "a fatalist," shaped by reason and sorrow more than ritual.

Yet during the Civil War—especially after losing his son Willie—his language changed.

He began to speak of God and Providence with increasing intimacy.

He read Scripture daily, quoting it in speeches that sounded more like sermons.

Then—almost a century later—came Ronald Reagan.

Baptized in the Disciples of Christ Church in Illinois, raised by a mother who filled his childhood with hymns and verses, Reagan often spoke as if America itself had a calling.

In 1983, he declared to the National Association of Evangelicals,

"If we forget that we are one nation under God, we will be a nation gone under."

Both men—Lincoln and Reagan—believed in the same unseen hand guiding history.

And yet, inside their own homes, another tension quietly brewed.

They were men who quoted Scripture. Men who publicly prayed. And still, behind closed doors, something wrestled between what they believed, what they would *tolerate*, and what they would even flirt with.

Lincoln's wife, Mary Todd, turned to mediums.

Reagan's wife, Nancy, turned to astrologers.

After the 1981 attempt on her husband's life, Nancy secretly began consulting astrologer Joan Quigley to plan his schedule. *"Astrology was simply another way of coping,"* she admitted years later.

And so, the pattern is impossible to ignore.

Two presidents who called on God.

Two first ladies who called on something else.

Each mixing light and shadow, faith and fear.

Now, you might think—Stevie, come on. At least they were spiritual. At least they believed in something.

But what if history shows that when *syncretism*—the blending of worship between God and other powers—enters a home, it never stays harmless?

What if it always starts as comfort…and ends in chaos?

Maybe it began with grief. Maybe with love.

But somewhere between the *séances* of 1863 and the *star charts* of 1983, the same door seemed to open again—the one the Bible calls forbidden. *And you have to wonder—when comfort crosses into communication with the wrong spirit…does it protect,*
or does it invite
something far more dangerous?

From the candles in Lincoln's Red Room to the *star charts* of Nancy Reagan, the thread doesn't snap—it evolves.

Every few decades, another leader reaches for the unseen.

Different eras, same hunger—to see what eyes can't.

You can call it curiosity.

Or you can call it a pattern.

Either way, the spiritual underworld of power has been hiding in **plain sight.**

From the candlelit tables of the Red Room—where presidents once gathered with *mediums* and whispered to the dead—our trail now leads to another table.

Another world.

Another era.

A table in Greece, near the ocean. The air heavy with salt, the kind of quiet that comes just before sunset. It wasn't a state dinner or a royal banquet. It was a meeting between a man and a psychic.

John Lennon—part of one of the most iconic bands in history, The Beatles—was not sitting with a radio host discussing his next album.

He was sitting with his wife…and a psychic, who began to read his palm.

That palm reading soon turned into something darker—what some would later call a prophecy.

He was told he would be killed on an island.

That he would die young.

Reports differ as to how he reacted. Some say he was shocked, even uneasy. Others say he shrugged it off, perhaps even laughed, treating it like a joke.

Because later in life, he would casually say things like, *"I'll probably just get shot by a looney fan."*

But as time would tell, there was nothing funny about what was coming.

Years later, Lennon was murdered in New York—young, just as foretold.

And though no one had imagined it then, one of his close friends would later reflect: *"We never thought of New York as an island—but it is. Surrounded by water."*

The prophecy had found its way home.

From that seaside table in Greece, we move to another table.

Another artist.

Another soul who may have spoken death into existence without realizing it.

Jimi Hendrix—one of the greatest guitar players to ever live—once sat with a tarot card reader.

The reader drew the Death Card, number 13.

Not long after, Hendrix began speaking about dying young. Those words left his mouth more than once.

Almost as if he was aligning himself with it—agreeing with the idea that he **wouldn't grow old, that**

The cards were already stacked against him.

And soon, he didn't.

Now let's shift the lens again.

From guitars and fame — to royalty.

Princess Diana.

A woman adored by millions around the world, the very image of grace and compassion.

If anyone looked like they lived a fairytale life—it was her.

And yet, the deeper you look, the darker the pages become.

It was later confirmed by her own attorneys that Diana feared someone was stalking her. She even wrote it down—letters that surfaced after her death—claiming that someone wanted to kill her, and that it might happen through a car accident.

No matter where you stand on conspiracy theories, that detail alone is chilling.

She died in a car crash, in a tunnel in Paris—the same way she said it would happen.

Premonition?

Or permission?

Because she's not alone.

Tupac Shakur—the rapper, poet, cultural revolutionary —said repeatedly that he believed he would die young. He talked about it in interviews, lyrics, and private conversations. Just weeks before his death, he released a song and music video showing himself in the afterlife—"I Ain't Mad at Cha."

Then, almost as if the prophecy demanded its fulfillment, he was gone.
Shot.
Young.

Was that a warning from heaven?

Or a spoken alignment with something darker?

And then, **Michael Jackson**.

The King of Pop.

He said it too—again and again—"They want me dead."

He said it on camera, on stage, and in interviews. His family later confirmed that he often spoke about being targeted, believing they would kill him for his music publishing rights. A close friend later claimed Jackson privately wrote **13** messages before his death, warning, "They are trying to murder me" and "I am scared about my life.

I remember watching some of those interviews years ago—before all this—and brushing it off as another celebrity being dramatic.

But now…looking back through the evidence, it's hard not to pause.

Was that paranoia?
Or prophecy?
Premonition—or permission?

Amy Winehouse—her raspy, soulful voice could cut through a room like smoke.

But behind that gift was a storm.

She often said she didn't think she'd live past a certain age. And her brother later confirmed in interviews that Amy used to speak that way—half joking, half believing it.

She died…young, just as she said she would.

By the way, this is only a fraction of the evidence I found. I was forced to cut back on names—celebrities, artists, even everyday people—whose own words seemed to predict their tragic deaths. The list is long enough to fill another book. Some of these additional case files will be available on my website for those who want to dig deeper.

Now—let's go from fame…to **power**.
President John F. Kennedy.
It's been reported that before his fatal trip to Texas, he told aides he didn't feel good about it.
That he felt doomed.
That he'd said more than once it would be easy for someone to shoot the president from a building.
Not long after, it happened exactly that way.
Did he dream it?
Did he sense it?
Was it fear speaking—or something trying to warn him?
And where were the pastors, ministers, and clergy who surrounded him?
Did no one stop to confront the words he was speaking?

Marilyn Monroe—who moved in the same orbit as JFK—was haunted by insomnia and a *preoccupation with death*. She confided to photographer André de Dienes that she *feared dying young* and staged photos in shadowed alleys and rooftops, reflecting a fascination with her own fragility. Her life, too, ended tragically and mysteriously—leaving more questions than answers. More info & sources in the bibliography section.

And then…we come to *Myles Munroe.*
A once-powerful spiritual leader, respected around the world.
He once said publicly—half-jokingly—that his plan was to die with his wife.
In a sermon that's still online today, he used an example of a plane crash, saying,
*"What if the Holy Spirit tried to wake someone up and tell them to pray for Brother Myles, but they just **hit the snooze button**—and then you hear Brother Myles died in a plane crash?"*

The congregation laughed.

But later, that's exactly what happened.

He and his wife died together—in a plane crash.

Which now brings us to the present.

Fourth quarter of 2025.

Charlie Kirk.

As I began trying to make sense of how a tragedy like that could happen, I started uncovering videos—some showing him recounting his experience meeting witches in New Mexico.

He described that region as *"one of the most pagan places in America."*

He said they approached him at a church, and that he became very sick afterward.

His words—not mine.

Then I kept watching.

I saw videos of him learning, growing, seeking truth—mentored by people from many spiritual walks of life.

I don't say that in judgment. I didn't know Charlie personally. Only God knows his heart. Only God knows his prayers. I'm just looking at the evidence.

None of this is written to question his faith, only to trace the language of fear that kept repeating.

Because one video after another, he kept repeating the same phrase: "They want me dead."

Maybe he said it for awareness.

Maybe to warn others.

But maybe—without realizing it—he didn't understand the spiritual power of agreement.

54 | Or maybe he did.

I don't know.

In text messages that later surfaced publicly online—none of which have been contested by anyone close to Charlie—it was revealed that he had spoken even more explicitly about his own sense of foreknowledge. Charlie described vivid, recurring dreams and referred to them as a "true prophecy." His exact words read:

"If I tell you the true prophecy that I know in my gut, it's really sad. But I hope it's wrong."

"Anyway I am not sure if I will live to see the end of this revolution."

"Since the beginning of TPUSA I knew in my gut that I might get wiped out at any time."

"I cannot explain it."

"But I dream about it all the time."

"Like all the time."

All I know is what's on the record.
At that point, I had to stop.
And really take in everything on the evidence board in front of me.
From the Red Room in the White House,
to the tarot table in Greece,
to mansions in Hollywood—
I saw the same spiritual crime repeating across time.
Different faces.

Different decades.

Same unseen pattern.

They were stalked.

Not by flesh and blood.

But by something else.

Look at the evidence.
- Fear.
- Premonition of tragedy.
- Words spoken—serious or joking—that became reality.
- Mixtures of faith and forbidden spirituality—talking to God and dabbling in the dark at the same time.

Those are the patterns.
Right there.
Hiding in plain sight.
And if that's true—if this invisible fingerprint keeps showing up across centuries,
across cultures,
across kings, presidents, prophets, and popstars—then what exactly are we looking at?
I felt it in my chest.
My heart pounding as I pinned the last picture on the board.

I knew there was something here—something big—but I couldn't quite touch it yet.

I didn't want to assume.

I didn't want to force conclusions.

I needed one more clue.

     And then—another piece of evidence arrived.

The kind that changes everything.

If any of this sounds unbelievable—or if your skepticism burns as hot as mine did when I first uncovered these patterns—every receipt is accounted for. And I promise you this: if you stick with me, by the time you reach the end, it will all make sense.

4

WORDS CREATE WORLDS

The Case Against Your Mouth

"Heaven keeps receipts — even for the words we swallow."

"Is it unethical to let him keep talking? Yes."
—from an article published by *Jezebel* Magazine,
September 2025

The bell rang, and the hallway erupted.

Hundreds of students poured out like a flood, sneakers squeaking, lockers slamming, voices bouncing off the tile. The smell of pencil shavings and cafeteria pizza hung in the air. I was carrying my bookbag from sewing class—yeah, sewing. A required class to graduate. Back then, it was part of "life skills." But that day, something heavier than fabric was being stitched together.

Ricky walked like he owned the hallway—basketball swagger, cheerleaders orbiting him like satellites, laughter always just a weapon away.

And then there was Jeff—the kid he picked on. Quiet, careful, clutching his books like a shield.

For three days straight, I watched Ricky shove, mock, and humiliate him.

Day one, I told myself it wasn't my business.

Day two, I told myself it would stop. Until it didn't.

By day three, I couldn't stomach it anymore.

I had a plan.

When the bell rang that afternoon, I stayed close. The crowd poured out again, a blur of backpacks and conversation. Just as I expected, Ricky shoved Jeff into the lockers, books scattering across the floor.

I dropped my bag and ran toward them.

The sound of my steps cut through the noise.

Before I knew it, Ricky was on the ground and the hallway had gone completely still.

I stood over him and said, calm but final:

"Leave him alone. One more move and I won't give you a warning."

The principal rushed in. Papers. Detention slips. Suspensions.

But Ricky never touched Jeff again.

It was worth it. Because I'll never forget the look on Jeff's face— that shock, that relief, that silent thank you. Even now, years later, I still remember.

That hallway taught me something simple but permanent:

When no one steps in, the bully writes the story.

And sometimes, the only righteous thing left to do…is condemn.

Maybe you've seen your own hallway—online, at work, or even in church. Maybe you've stood there, watching the shove, hearing the laughter, telling yourself it's not your fight.

Which brings me to something else that needs condemning.

Not scandals.
Not politics.

Words.

Because sometimes evil doesn't break bones—it builds narratives. And if no one challenges the narrative, the hallway just gets bigger.

Every tragedy begins with a sentence.

Every war starts with a whisper.

Every curse starts with agreement.

We're asking the question that echoes through every headline:

Where was God?

But to even begin answering that question, we have to look at what God says about Himself.

Because before we can accuse Heaven of silence,

We have to remember how Heaven speaks.

God didn't just describe Himself with titles—He identified Himself with words.

"In the beginning was the Word…"

But before we go there…

Let's look at the cultural story everyone's still talking about—and connect the dots.

Some called Charlie Kirk a political pundit.

Others called him an evangelist.

For many, he was family.

Now, you don't have to be political.

You don't even have to like the guy.

But we can all agree on this:

A husband.

A father.

A son—publicly executed.

That should never be acceptable.

Violence should never get the last word.

Charlie Kirk wasn't murdered because he threw a punch.

He was assassinated because he wouldn't stop talking.

He was a debater in an age of silence—a man who still believed in the power of words when most people only believed in algorithms.

He showed up, face-to-face, word-for-word, while others hid behind screens.

The shirt he wore that day said one word: FREEDOM.

Bold letters printed across his chest.

But the thing that killed him…wasn't just a bullet.

Words that cursed.

Words that whispered.

Words that lied.

Words that went unchallenged.

And I wonder, did anyone serve notice?

Did anyone confront the evil words being spewed? | 61

I don't mean the kind of words that make you uncomfortable because of politics.

No.

I mean evil words, words of violence, words of death, words designed to destroy.

Threats spoken out loud.

Agreements whispered in darkness.

Sentences that sounded like jokes but landed like spells.

Because here's the truth:

If words can start wars…words can also stop them.

If words can curse…they can also cancel the curse.

So let's trace the evidence not to assign blame, but to expose a pattern.

Because behind every visible tragedy…there's usually an invisible sentence that started it.

And the more you trace it, the more you realize—those sentences aren't buried in mystery.

They're right in front of us.

Hiding in articles.

Trending in headlines.

Masquerading as jokes that get shared a million times.

We have to go there.

Yeah—that magazine.

The one that bragged about hiring witches to curse him.

I mentioned it earlier—but it deserves a closer look now.

Because in case you missed the irony, there really was a queen in Scripture—a witch-queen who threatened prophets and tried to silence the voices of truth.

Her name was Jezebel.

You can't make this stuff up.

And that's when my investigation hit a wall.

A spiritual one.

Because forty-eight hours before Charlie was shot, his family was already living under unnecessary fear—with stress, threats, whispers of witchcraft, and money changing hands.

It was all there.

Eerily familiar.

A modern echo of an ancient script.

The Bible records a similar moment:

> "So Jezebel sent a messenger to Elijah, saying, 'May the gods deal with me, be it ever so severely, if by this time tomorrow I do not make your life like one of them.'" (1 Kings 19:2 NIV).

A death threat.

Just words—but words that made a prophet run.

So I kept looking for something I couldn't find.

Any clip. Any prayer. Any voice saying:

"In the name of Jesus, I break every word curse. I bind every hex. I cancel every spiritual contract made in darkness."

But it wasn't there.

And then I remembered the verse everyone quotes:

"No weapon formed against you shall prosper" (Isaiah 54:17 NKJV).

But the part we forget says:

"And every tongue which rises against you in judgment you shall condemn."

Let that sink in.

Not your pastor.

Not your priest.

You.

Contracts fascinate me. Precision matters.

So that word *condemn* stopped me cold.

It's not poetry.

It's legal.

To condemn means to declare something unfit for use—like a city posting "Unsafe Structure" on a building before demolition. If something is condemned, it's scheduled for destruction.

And maybe that's what Isaiah meant all along:

If you don't condemn the tongue, the weapon might prosper.

Not because God failed—but because He honors your jurisdiction.

That mix of truth and questions haunted me.

And it brought back a memory I hadn't thought about in years.

That hallway.

That fight.

| 63

That moment I realized evil thrives when no one steps in.

Silence isn't neutrality.

It's permission.

So I started searching deeper. Not just for proof—but for pattern. Because patterns tell stories, and the story didn't end with Charlie.

Princess Diana.

Tupac Shakur.

John Lennon.

JFK.

Different decades, same script.

Fear.

Premonition.

Confession.

Words that foreshadowed their own deaths.

Could that really be coincidence?

Or are we witnessing the oldest law in existence—the law of words?

I turned back to Scripture.

"Death and life are in the power of the tongue" (Proverbs 18:21 NKJV).

"For thing I greatly feared has come upon me" (Job 3:25 NKJV).

"He will have whatever he says" (Mark 11:23 NKJV).

Every verse, the same pattern: speech creates structure.

Language builds reality.

What if words are spiritual contracts? What if Heaven responds to faith the way gravity responds to motion?

It doesn't matter who jumps—the law works.

Still, not every wound fits neatly into this framework. There are tragedies that leave no trail of words—storms, earthquakes, losses that seem to strike without warning. Some corners of suffering remain shrouded in mystery, the kind that drives us to faith, not formulas. Even so, the truth still stands:

And if that's the case…then silence is still participation.

Every unchallenged lie becomes a seed.

Every idle word, a legal agreement waiting for someone to cancel it.

That's when the dots connected.

In the beginning was the Word.

And the Word was with God.

And the Word was God. —John 1:1 NKJV

Of all the titles He could've chosen—King, Judge, Commander—He chose Word.

Because when God wanted to redeem the world, He didn't send a sword.

He sent a sentence.

A Word that healed, silenced storms, and raised the dead.

A Word that rewrote the verdict of humanity.

If God's identity is wrapped in being the Word…
then what we speak isn't trivial.
It's jurisdictional.
It's creative.
It's binding.
And for those of us who say,
"Hey, I'm not confrontational. It's all peace, man. It's all love."
That's cool.

But what if I told you that God even cares about the words you refuse to say?

"But I say to you that for every idle word that men may speak, they will give account of it in the day of judgment. For by your words you will be justified, and by your words you will be condemned" (Matthew 12:36–37 NKJV).

Idle word?

In the original Greek, the word used is *argos*—it means inactive, barren, unproductive, without work.

Literally: a word that could have done something…but didn't.

So when Jesus said we'll give account for every idle word, He wasn't just talking about gossip or profanity—He was talking about wasted authority.

Unspoken truth.

Unused power.

Words that could have healed, defended, blessed, or canceled darkness…but sat silent instead.

Could it be that on Judgment Day, God won't just ask what we said—He'll ask about what we refused to say?

Almost like a courtroom witness who never took the stand.

An idle witness. | 65

A silent believer who saw injustice, felt the prompting, but stayed quiet.

Maybe those idle words will rise as evidence.

Maybe Heaven will say,

"You stood by. You didn't say anything.

You stood by. You didn't pray.

You stood by—and you didn't use the authority I gave you."

Because silence isn't peace.

It's partnership.

And every word—spoken or idle—is still on the record.

Which brings me back to those parties and summer barbecues when I was a kid—faith leaders from every denomination circling our table, my father hosting, breaking bread, swapping stories, debating miracles. They'd shake hands at the end and plan the next one. That was normal. But looking back now, I wonder: did we miss it? Did someone have a truth that could have changed the outcome, but it went unspoken?

History is littered with patterns. JFK surrounded by priests. Myles Munroe by pastors. Michael Jackson raised in church. John Lennon hearing psychics tell him his "expiration date." Amy Winehouse singing her own funeral soundtrack. Different decades, same undertone: evil whispering a script, people repeating it, and almost no one stepping in to cancel the story.

And if that's true, then we have to ask: where was the Church? Not the cathedral, but the *ekklesia*—the governing body Jesus described. The one He said would storm the gates of hell. The one He handed the keys to. The one with authority over all the power of the enemy.

What would have happened if Michael Jackson had bumped into a man or woman who actually believed in GOD—ON—EARTH level of authority? If a Secret Service agent had told JFK about a different script?

From the biblical perspective, the question of authority isn't theoretical. Jesus already settled it.

Jesus said His followers would do even greater works than He did. He promised that nothing would by any means harm them and that the gates of evil wouldn't stand. That's authority—not a slogan, but a legal right. The same way you'd step in and shut down a vicious lie about your spouse, your child, or your best friend, you're called to stand up and confront every false word, every dark narrative, and cancel it. That's what condemning means. That's what using your spiritual authority looks like.

So I have to wonder: Are we still telling ourselves "it's not my fight" while the bully goes unchecked? Are we still dressing passivity in God's will and calling it holiness?

Because if words create worlds…then silence writes its own story too.

And the story we've been telling ourselves—the one we've tolerated, excused, or spiritualized—might be the very thing allowing the enemy to keep writing chapters that were never in God's original script.

So maybe it wasn't just silence. Perhaps it was something more subtle. Agreement, dressed as reverence. Inaction, disguised as surrender. A quiet nod to tragedy…while calling it God's timing.

And that's when another question started to haunt me.

Of all the creatures God made—every lion that roars, every whale that sings, every bird that echoes through the trees—why did He give only humans the ability to form words?

To speak.

To create sound joined to consciousness.

Why?

Myles Munroe, the faith leader who taught a generation about the power of words and divine purpose, often reminded people that language wasn't random—it was responsibility. God could have made humanity stronger, faster, or more instinctive than the animals. Instead, He made us vocal.

He gave us speech—the power to name, to declare, to decree.

And that realization hit me hard.

Because as I kept investigating, something shifted in me.

I was no longer just studying a crime scene for fingerprints of the enemy—I was starting to look for the missing evidence of responsibility.

Maybe the real story wasn't just about an attacker, but about those who had authority to intervene…and didn't.

The people who could have locked the door before evil walked in—but didn't bother to get up.

In an age of indifference, silence can look like innocence.

But maybe it's complicity.

That realization sent me digging deeper—beyond the headlines, beyond the history books—into the very beginning.

The verse that cracked the case open for me was the one that's been hiding in plain sight since Genesis:

"Let us make man in our image, after our likeness: and let them have dominion over…the earth" (Genesis 1:26 KJV).

Dominion.

Authority.

Agency.

Myles Munroe once taught that this verse wasn't just theology—it was jurisdiction. He taught that Heaven would never override human authority on earth. That if humanity stayed silent, Heaven would stay still.

Ironically, he preached those truths with passion—then years later died in a plane crash after illustrating that very principle: saying that if people failed to rise up and lead, God would not be able to intervene…

It was only an example—but the outcome was tragically literal.

That connection rattled me.

It felt less like coincidence and more like a trail of divine breadcrumbs leading toward a bigger truth.

So I had to ask the next question—one that still echoes through every tragedy, every unanswered prayer, every "where was God?" moment:

If God gave humanity dominion over the earth…

did He also intentionally limit Himself?

Now stay with me.

Because if that's true—if Heaven waits for alignment instead of overriding it—

then the next story in Scripture suddenly feels less like ancient history and more like a case study.

A moment where one man's agreement with God shifted the outcome of an entire nation.

Go back with me in history—to a showdown between witches and a prophet.

The scene wasn't a stadium or a studio, but a mountaintop. The prophets under Jezebel's spell weren't strumming guitars or holding microphones—they were holding knives. They cut themselves to be seen. To prove their gods were real. The air was thick with chants, smoke, and blood.

Jezebel had 850 prophets under her influence. Four-hundred-fifty showed up that day on Mount Carmel. Elijah stood alone—one prophet aligned with Heaven against hundreds echoing lies.

Heaven didn't need noise. It needed alignment.

Jezebel's prophets were loud, frenzied—slashing and shouting to be seen. Fire fell because Heaven found harmony.

On that mountain, it wasn't just noise that filled the air. It was blood. Jezebel's prophets cut themselves, smearing the altar with their own lives to prove their gods were real. Elijah, on the other hand, rebuilt the Lord's altar, drenched it in water, and trusted Heaven to answer for Himself.

Two altars. Two sources of power. Same pattern: whenever the spirit world is in play, blood is never far from the scene.

And that raised another question I couldn't shake:

Why does blood seem to matter so much?

Did you know the Bible says blood speaks?

That burning question took me to another crime scene.
One buried under centuries of silence.
The first murder in history.
One brother against another.

Cain and Abel.
It's the first time the word *sin* ever appears in Scripture:
"Sin is crouching at your door…but you must rule over it" (Genesis 4:7 NIV).
But Cain didn't.
He opened the door instead.
And when he killed Abel, something happened that shook Heaven itself.
God said,
"The voice of your brother's blood cries out to Me from the ground" (Genesis 4:10 NKJV).
That line stopped me cold.
The blood had a voice?

Even in death…it spoke.

And suddenly, it made sense—why every religion, every witch, every priest, every ancient altar seems obsessed with blood.
Voodoo doctors look for chicken blood.

Pagans spill animal blood.

Israel's priests sprinkled lamb's blood.

Because blood isn't just biology—it's testimony.

The blood speaks.

So I started tracing the pattern.
Abel's blood cries for justice.
Christ's blood calls for mercy.
And I realized…this isn't poetry.
It's legal language.
And that's when I noticed something hidden in plain sight—a pattern that ran deeper than prophecy, deeper than power.
Because God doesn't just call Himself the Word.
He also calls Himself the Judge of all the earth.
One speaks creation into existence.
The other protects it from collapsing under corruption.
It's the same voice — one that builds, one that defends.
The same Word that spoke light into the darkness now sits on the bench to make sure darkness never has the final say.
Suddenly, Mount Carmel wasn't just a miracle scene.
It was a courtroom.
Evidence. Verdict. Fire as the gavel.
Heaven had rendered judgment in public view—not to prove ego, but to prove truth.
That revelation led me straight into another memory—one that had nothing to do with temples or sacrifices, but everything to do with law.
As a businessman, I've sat in more courtrooms than I ever cared to.
Business deals and the zip codes changed, but rules that govern judicial conduct remain.
There are laws every courtroom must honor, ethics every judge must uphold. If a judge becomes too close to one side—if there's even the appearance of bias—that judge must step down. It's called a motion to recuse. Because once a judge is compromised, justice collapses.

I once had a civil case where the judge turned out to be friends with the opposing attorney. Imagine sitting there, realizing the man holding your future in his gavel already shares coffee with your adversary. We filed the motion. Why? Because justice can't share coffee with corruption. Even the appearance of conflict disqualifies the bench.

That experience made me understand something I'd missed for years in Scripture. The rituals, the sacrifices, the blood, the tents— it was never random religion. It was legal protocol. Heaven's way of maintaining integrity in the universe's highest court.

Because there was another Judge—perfect, incorruptible, bound by His own Word.

And this Judge faced a case far more personal than mine.

His own children had been accused of the highest crime in existence: rebellion.

The charge? Murder of innocence.

The evidence? Overwhelming.

The first human family became the first crime scene.

Exhibit A: Abel's blood—crying out for justice.

That one act became a pattern. Every war, every betrayal, every act of violence added to the file. Billions of Exhibits, all logged into the cosmic record. And standing before the Judge was the Prosecutor—tireless, articulate, vicious.

Daniel 7:25 NKJV says he would "speak pompous words against the Most High, shall persecute the saints of the Most High, and shall intend to change times and law." Revelation 12:10 NKJV calls him "the accuser of our brethren, who accused them before our God day and night."

That's his strategy.

The same being who lured humanity into sin now prosecutes them for committing it.

Seduce, then accuse.

If you've ever met someone who tempts you toward ruin only to condemn you afterward—you've met his reflection.

The Judge, however, was trapped by His own perfection.

He longed to be near His children again, but the law He authored for their protection now indicted them. To simply dismiss the crime would shatter the moral fabric of creation. If He bent the rules for love's sake, the Accuser could call Him corrupt—a biased Judge unfit to rule. Heaven itself would file a motion to recuse Him.

So the Judge—in this case, God Himself—seems to have done something unthinkable.

Instead of scrapping the plan and walking away from humanity, He seems to have written an exception. A clause that let mercy breathe inside the system.

What if life itself became the language of appeal—a temporary bridge between the guilty and the good? The blood of animals began to mean something more than loss. It became a symbol, evidence that repentance still mattered. Maybe it was less about punishment, and more about proximity—a legal way for the Creator to visit His creation without violating His own justice.

That's why priests built tents, altars, and veils. Not to cage God, but to localize His holiness until justice could be permanently satisfied.

But every workaround eventually expires.

The blood of bulls could only postpone the case, not close it.

Every drop of sacrifice still testified: Justice owed.

Creation itself was contaminated with the evidence.

"Blood defiles the land, and no atonement can be made…except by the blood of him who shed it" (Numbers 35:33 NKJV).

This wasn't mere ritual; it was law. Innocent blood leaves a record, and creation itself seems to demand an answer.

Then—history's greatest twist.

The Judge stepped down from the bench.

He took the stand Himself.

He bore the sentence the law demanded.

At the Cross, the Judge became the Defendant.

"The blood of sprinkling that speaks better things than that of Abel" (Hebrews 12:24 NKJV).

Abel's blood cried justice owed.

Christ's blood declared justice paid.

It wasn't poetry. It was precedent.

When Jesus exhaled, "It is finished," the courtroom fell silent.

The veil—the heavenly restraining order—tore from top to bottom.

The verdict was rendered. Access granted.

The Accuser lost standing in Heaven's court—but perhaps that's why he still roams the earth, like a disbarred attorney desperate to twist testimony, distort evidence, and delay a sentence he knows is already sealed.

For the first time since Eden, the Judge could sit with His children again—not in a temple, not behind a curtain, but heart to heart.

No more mediators.

No more rituals.

No more visitation hours in a cosmic jail.

The Spirit who once hovered over prophets now moved into people—fishermen, teenagers, mothers, fathers, business owners.

The same power that once rested on a few now resided in a family.

Could this be the moment Joel saw centuries earlier—the prophecy Peter later repeated?

"In the last days...I will pour out My Spirit on all flesh; and your sons and your daughters shall prophesy" (Joel 2:28 KJV).

The same Spirit that once visited tents now inhabited temples of skin.

Could this be what the prophets longed for—God not just visiting, but moving in?

Maybe this was it. The prophecy fulfilled. The Judge coming home.

Maybe PENTECOST wasn't only about power, but about permission. Legal standing.

So what if the Cross wasn't only about saving humanity from sin—but releasing Heaven through humanity?

Because in the Old Testament, no one dared to call themselves a son or daughter of God. That kind of language could get you killed. God was distant, sacred, untouchable. Then Jesus came and changed the vocabulary. He called God Father. And for that, they accused Him of blasphemy.

But that word *Father* wasn't rebellion.

It was revelation.

Jesus wasn't just claiming sonship for Himself, but opening the door for the rest of the family.

The Cross didn't just forgive debts—it signed adoption papers.

The blood wasn't just shed as payment for sin—it was ink that signed the power of attorney over to the kids.

Ordinary people becoming living temples.

Maybe that was the plan all along.

That the same Spirit who hovered over chaos in Genesis would one day fill the lungs of humanity with the breath of God. | 73

That prophecy—the ability to speak what Heaven says—wasn't supposed to be a rare phenomenon, but a family trait.

Paul the Apostle later wrote to the Corinthians, urging them, "Desire spiritual gifts, but especially that you may prophesy" (1 Corinthians 14:1 NKJV). He wasn't writing to pastors or prophets—he was writing to bakers, farmers, merchants, parents, children.

He was telling ordinary people to desire the extraordinary—to see, hear, and speak what Heaven sees, hears, and speaks.

Is this the divine scandal? The Spirit that spoke through Elijah now lives in you. The same voice that called Lazarus out of the grave can whisper through your lungs. **The Cross didn't just free you from sin—it freed your speech. It made your tongue a tool of Heaven.**

That should make us stop.

If that's true, then every believer has the authority to counter hell's prophecies. To condemn every curse that's been spoken. To interrupt every demonic sentence with a divine comma. To rewrite what the enemy intended for harm with what Heaven intends for healing.

That was my turning point. The moment I stopped chasing words and started carrying them.

And from that day on, I understood: prophecy isn't about performance. It's about alignment. It's not magic—it's resonance. When you speak what God says, you amplify Heaven. When you repeat what fear says, you amplify hell.

Could it be that the tongue is a tuning fork—one that decides which kingdom gets amplified?

Our words might be more than noise; maybe they're signatures in the spiritual realm—co-signatures of Heaven or hell.

And God's promise through Joel still hangs in the air: Sons and daughters, young and old, will prophesy.

But what if prophecy isn't reserved for a stage or a ministry title?

What if we're all holding the mic—every time we open our mouths?

Could it be that we are all, in some way, our own closest prophet—whether for good or for ruin?

Could it be that JFK's premonitions, or Lincoln's dreams, or Amy Winehouse's lyrics weren't just artistic moments—but prophetic leaks?

Could it be that in some deeper, even more sinister way, whatever compelled them to speak the way they did might have tipped the scale between Heaven's intervention and hell's permission?

You don't need a stage. You don't need someone else's permission.

If the Spirit lives in you, you already carry God's microphone.

The Spirit didn't come to visit you. He came to voice through you.

Because every time you open your mouth, you're choosing your harmony.

Heaven or hell.

"For every action, there is an equal and opposite reaction."
— Newton's Third Law

So if the Bible is true—and if the evil one really does stand as the accuser in the courtroom of Heaven—then maybe the Creator Himself has placed the gavel in our hands.

Not to recite seven positive affirmations from the latest self-help trend, but to legally condemn every evil word spoken against us.

Because if that's true, then the implications are staggering.

It would mean that in that courtroom, silence isn't harmless; it's agreement.

Every unchallenged word becomes a seed, and what we refuse to spiritually condemn, we empower.

Like Newton's law, maybe every action in the spirit demands a reaction.

Every curse might require a counter.

Every lie could be waiting for someone bold enough to strike it from the record.

And if that's true, it means your mouth might be writing tomorrow's headlines.

Pause.

Maybe it's time to look in the mirror.

Have any words been spoken over you—by someone else, or by your own voice—that still echo in the dark?

Have tragic stories been looping in your head so long that they started to sound like truth?

What if you've been waiting for someone else to fix what God already gave you the power to condemn?

Because if this courtroom is real, silence is not innocence.

It's participation by omission.

You don't win cases by staying quiet. | 75

You have to speak.

You have to act.

If God takes words so seriously—if He records every idle sentence, every whisper, every agreement—then maybe our silence isn't neutral either.

Maybe even the things we never said are still waiting to be addressed.

Maybe Heaven's courtroom doesn't just archive the noise we make…

but the words we were too afraid to say.
And if that's true—
if every phrase, every promise, every avoided truth leaves a trace—
then it would mean only one thing:

"Heaven keeps receipts—even for the words we swallow."

5

GHOSTS, KEYS, & GRACE

Where Grace Meets the War

"For we wrestle not against flesh and blood...
—Ephesians 6:12 KJV

The phone rang.

"Hey Stevie, good news," Nick said. "The owner's ready to make a deal."

And just like that, this moment would trigger one of the most bizarre chapters of my life.

See, about ten years earlier, I had decided I was done with God.

Done with Christian music. Done with the stage, the microphones, the endless smiles that hid private wounds.

I wasn't angry; I was numb. Tired of praying for other people's miracles while watching my own never come. Tired of being the guy who poured out faith only to go home empty.

So I did what made sense to me at the time—

I quit God

I ran.

Running as far away from God and ministry as I possibly could, I started building my own empire—my way.

Have you ever found yourself running from God? Or maybe blaming Him for what other people did to you? For the doors that never opened, the people who never came back, the dreams that didn't make it past the starting line?

Yeah. That was me.

I made a quiet promise that I would never be disappointed again. Never depend on anyone again.

And if I couldn't trust Heaven, I'd trust the hustle.

So, ten years later, I was on the cusp of something big. The dreamer in me had turned into a businessman, and the businessman in me didn't hesitate. When I saw opportunity, I moved.

I told Nick, "Send the paperwork. Let's do the deal."

I was already seeing dollar signs in my head.

This was the next chapter of my entrepreneurial story. I'd owned multiple businesses in different industries, but this one—this one was going to be special.

The pet industry was exploding across the country. The pandemic had changed everything. People were lonely, adopting dogs and cats they called their "fur babies."

The market was massive. I didn't even need to pray about it. I just did the math. Once I saw what my competitors were making, I didn't think twice.

I bought the web domain, inked the company, and launched what I believed would become the next national chain of high-end pet hotels and spas.

At that point, God, spiritual warfare, and callings were the last thing on my mind.

I wasn't chasing revival—I was chasing revenue. And I told myself that this time, I was finally in control.

After a few weeks of negotiation, the contracts were finally signed.

The big day had come.

It was supposed to be a family thing. My mother- and father-in-law were visiting from Europe, so everyone piled into the SUV. We woke up at five a.m. on a Saturday for the four-hour drive south.

The building was sight unseen—I'd only studied the photos, the comps, the specs online—but I knew one thing: we were headed straight into one of the wealthiest, most population-dense pockets of Florida.

Palm trees. Yachts. Boca Raton.

The building was just a few minutes from the yacht club.

I wasn't nervous.

I'd already interviewed staff, even hired one of the best groomers in the state—a dog whisperer who could calm a pit bull with a glance.

Everything was clicking.

Marketing was my lane, and I knew exactly how to turn a property into profit.

By the time we hit Broward County, I was already planning ad campaigns in my head.

We had customers on a waiting list before the doors even opened.

When we finally rolled into Boca, the whole car went quiet.

Mansions lined the water; sailboats tilted in the morning light.

Endless possibilities.

Then we turned into the lot.

The family gave a collective "whoa."

The place looked straight out of the *Addams Family*—part gothic, part forgotten psych ward.

Weeds everywhere.

Grass up to your knees, a faded green-gray paint job that looked allergic to sunlight.

Still, all I saw were dollar signs.

A couple coats of paint, new signage, and we'd be off to the races.

Three cars waited in the lot: two real-estate agents and the woman who'd managed the previous pet hospital for over a decade.

That's when I learned the odd part—the hospital wasn't relocating across town or even across county lines. They were moving across the street.

They'd just spent close to a hundred grand remodeling the reception area, a marble-floored showpiece that looked like a plastic-surgery lobby.

Why walk away now?

Red flag number one.

But I ignored it.

Everyone wanted this deal to close fast. We were doing a lease with an option to buy, and all parties were "motivated," as Nick put it.

I told my family to wait in the car.

I stepped inside.

The front lobby gleamed; the rest of the place did not. Beyond the reception counter, the corridors narrowed into something that felt |81 more like a maze than a clinic. Cold steel tables, dim fluorescent lights, equipment that looked like it belonged in a different decade.

Then I saw it—a large freezer.

I asked what it was for.

The manager said matter-of-factly, "That's where they kept the cadavers—dogs that were put down."

She asked if I wanted to keep it.

I told her she could take it on her way out.

At the back of the first floor stretched a long hallway lined with built-in kennels—hundreds of cages, small to large. Cold steel, stacked like drawers in a morgue.

It was just business to them, but something about it made me feel like the building carried a story it didn't want to tell.

We climbed the stairs. The air felt heavier up there, like the atmosphere changed mid-landing.

The second floor had real potential—balcony, ocean breeze, offices with light spilling in through dust-coated blinds. Rumor was the doctor who once ran the place had lived upstairs while performing surgeries downstairs.

Creepy, but convenient.

Either way, I could already see new carpet, fresh drywall, bright signage. Problem solved.

We came back down, retracing that long hallway toward the front lobby.

That's when I noticed the woman's expression.

Professional smile, but something behind it—like words trying to escape.

"Is there anything else you want to tell me about the building?" I asked. Honestly, I wasn't fishing for anything deep. I figured she might want to explain how the alarm system worked, or where the breaker panel was. Business stuff.

Instead, she hesitated, pressed her lips together, and said words I never expected to hear in the middle of a real-estate deal.

"You should get yourself a priest."

So I cleared my throat.

Honestly, I thought she was either joking or trying to scare me out of the deal—maybe a tactic to keep me from opening a competing business across the street. But then I remembered: they'd been a hospital, and we were a high-end spa. If anything, our businesses complemented each other.

So what was her angle?

"What did you say?" I asked again.

She looked me dead in the eye and repeated,

"You might want to call a priest."

At that moment, the color drained from the faces of the two real-estate agents who had been tagging. You could almost feel them tiptoe backward, inch by inch, toward the exit while pretending not to.

The air in that lobby thickened as if someone had turned off the oxygen.

I told her it was okay—mostly to calm the room. I was the only man there, and there was no way I was going to act spooked. "Please, tell me more. Why do I need to call a priest?"

She nodded, like she had been waiting for permission. Then she unloaded years of stories.

For as long as she'd worked there, strange things kept happening— Doctors claimed they saw shadows where no one stood.

Staff on overnight shifts saying they heard footsteps and doors slamming upstairs when the second floor was empty.

Lights flicking on and off without reason.

And, she said, sometimes the children—patients' kids who tagged along—talked about "friends" they saw in the hallways.

Imaginary friends, she called them at first, until she wasn't so sure they were imaginary.

Then she told me, but it's OK don't worry about it. They are friendly spirits. I thought to myself that didn't make much sense. If they were friendly, why were people so terrorized, and why were they moving across the street instead of staying in the building.

By this point, I was half skeptic and half believer. I'd grown up in church. I'd seen my father cast demons out of people while I sat behind a piano.

But a building itself? I'd never heard of a structure carrying some kind of spiritual residue.

I thanked her for the information, even smiled to keep it professional. The real-estate agents said goodbye, and bolted for the parking lot—like bats out of hell. | 83

The manager said she'd leave out the back since her car was parked there.

She pressed the building keys into my hand—the metal cold against my palm—and for the first time that day, my excitement cracked.

I didn't sign up for this. I didn't want this kind of drama. I wanted a simple, profitable deal, something peaceful enough that maybe I could stay overnight upstairs when I was in town. But as she walked away, I felt the optimism drain out of me. I told myself it didn't matter.

Whatever, I thought. I'm here to make money.

I followed her toward the back exit door, maybe six feet between us. Dim light, dust in the air, a little sunlight sneaking through the narrow windows.

That's when it happened.

A small object rolled hard across the floor—fast, deliberate, almost playful. It came from an open room on my right, crossed between her and me, and tapped the far wall like a warning shot. It wasn't heavy, but it wasn't random either. Whatever pushed it wanted to be noticed.

I froze.

Looked down.

Thought, You've got to be kidding me.

Maybe I was overthinking. Maybe adrenaline was making me see things.

Still, the ball sat there.

We reached the back door; I forced a grin. "Nice meeting you. Good luck with the new place..

She echoed the same and slipped out into the daylight.

Then I turned the lock, keys rattling in my hand. For the first time, I realized I had officially taken possession. The building was mine.

And yet, standing in that hallway, I couldn't shake the feeling that I wasn't alone.

I had a flashback...

There was another hallway once—different building, different time.

Back in Chapter 4, I had been the hero in that hallway. I'd stepped in to defend a stranger and took down a bully twice my size.

That hallway had witnesses, blood pressure, adrenaline.

This one?

This one had silence.

The enemy here didn't have a face.

Little did I know, this place would become a prophetic mirror to my own life.

Because the truth is, I was haunted too—by my past, my bitterness, by every could've and should've that replayed in my head. Haunted by guilt, regret, and shadows of the people who hurt me...

Still, I was a tough guy.

Nothing scared me.

I'd wrestled in middle school and high school. Hours of drills, takedowns, headlocks, overpowering my opponents, and pinning their backs flat to the mat. I knew how to win hand-to-hand combat.

But that muscle memory couldn't help me here.

Whatever this was, it was invisible.

And I felt it.

I cleared my throat and muttered to myself, "Well, here we are." The dream was mine now. Keys in hand, profit on paper, but something felt wrong.

I walked back toward the wall where the ball had come from.

Still there.

Not imagination.

I pulled out my phone, snapped a picture—evidence, I told myself.

You might think I'm exaggerating, making it sound more mysterious than it was. But as sure as my name is Stevie, it happened.

Truth be told, I was so far from God that praying didn't even cross my mind. Heaven felt closed for business.

I locked the front door, stepped out into the heat, and told my family, "Let's grab lunch. We'll come back later."

The family wondered why I didn't look as celebratory as I probably should have looked.

Here I was, taking over a building already zoned for my specific type of business, one of a kind in that area. The licenses were ready. The customers were ready. Money wasn't the problem. Everything about this moment said I should be grinning from ear to ear.

I told my wife, *I'll tell you later.*

I was trying to be discreet.

Isn't it interesting that sometimes moments that should be celebratory feel strangely heavy? Like something's standing in the corner of your joy, trying to drain the color out of it.

That's exactly how I felt.

So, we sat at Chili's—me, my wife, her parents—and I told them quietly what the woman at the building had said. I kept my tone low. I didn't need strangers at the next table thinking I'd lost it.

We finished eating, paid the bill, and headed back toward my new investment.

I'd be lying if I told you I wasn't apprehensive about taking my family into that place. But I told myself to shake it off. Maybe the lady was dramatic. Maybe she wanted to sabotage the deal. Maybe I was overthinking.

We'd checked into a hotel near the beach. The sun was out, palm trees swaying like everything was normal. I kept repeating in my head: This is just business. Nothing else.

When we pulled up, I unlocked the door and flipped on every switch I could find, but the light still felt dim.

Not dark in color—dark in weight.

Both of my dogs were with me—Zara, calm and quiet, and Picasso, my Jack Russell terrier. We called him Pico for short, and when he got extra feisty, Pico de Gallo.

Little dog, big attitude. The kind that thought he could fight bears.

But that day, my fearless dog wanted nothing to do with the building.

Maybe it was the scent of old anesthesia or years of fear baked into the tile. Later I learned it had once been an OB-GYN clinic before becoming a vet hospital in the '70s. Maybe he sensed something I couldn't.

All I know is his tail stood straight up, the hair on his neck standing to attention—like a row of tiny daggers down his spine—eyes locked on a distant room I hadn't even noticed.

He wouldn't follow me. He barked, paced, whined—low and uneasy. It wasn't his usual "let's play fetch" bark. It was protective, primal.

I tried to stay calm. *Get what you need, Stevie. Wrap it up. Head home.*

86 |

The manager I'd hired, Peter, hadn't seen any of this. He was scheduled to arrive later that afternoon to pick up the keys and prep for opening day.

And I figured—why tell him? If I told him what had happened, he'd either quit or walk around scared, seeing shadows that weren't there.

So I kept my mouth shut. Only my family and the real-estate agents knew what went down that morning.

Maybe whatever was there would just…leave.

Pack its bags and move on.

Peter showed up later, all optimism and energy. The kind of guy who could sell snow to a snowman. Tough, bearded former New Englander—looked like he could wrestle a gator for fun.

I gave him a pep talk, acted like nothing strange had happened, handed him the keys, and headed home with my family.

Day 1: smooth.

Day 2: still smooth.

By Day 5, I was back on the other side of the state, sitting at the kitchen table with a cold soda when my phone buzzed.

"Hey boss, either I'm nuts or we got ghost pets in the salon."

The text was from Peter.

He had no clue about the woman's warning. He'd never met her. He didn't know a single person connected to the deal.

And yet here we were.

So, like any good CEO who's been away from God for a decade, I went into damage-control mode. "Probably the A/C," I texted back. "Nothing to worry about. I'll have maintenance check it." Then I gave him a pep talk worthy of a TED Talk and told him to get back to work.

But just like President Reagan once said—trust, but verify.

I opened my CCTV app. Twelve live feeds. I tapped the front-desk camera. There he was: Peter, alone, finishing his sub sandwich.

Then—he drops it.

Shoots out of his chair.

Spins around like he's chasing a sound that doesn't exist.

You can see him mouthing words, pointing, circling the room.

No audio. Just silent panic.

And that's when it hit me:

Whatever was in that building wasn't leaving quietly. |87

I couldn't wish it away.

Couldn't out-market it.

Couldn't drown it in ambition or caffeine.

So, I did the only thing a man who'd been running from God for ten years could think to do.

I called my Pentecostal mom.

I told her what had happened, and I could almost hear her breathing slow on the other side of the line. She didn't panic, but she didn't shrug it off either. She just said, "We're going to pray." That was her default mode for anything she couldn't fix with her own hands.

Since she was over two thousand miles away, she told my dad what was happening, and the two of them reached out to one of our old evangelist friends, Ricky. Not the same Ricky from my teenage days, but another one. A real-deal spiritual street fighter. The type of man who didn't need a microphone to cast something out; his presence alone shifted the air.

I told him what was going on and he laughed softly, not mockingly—more like someone who'd seen worse. "You wouldn't believe the things I've seen in ministry," he said.

We agreed to meet soon, but life and travel got in the way. Weeks turned into months, and every time I thought it was the day we'd go in there together, something would come up.

Within six months, I only went back a handful of times—get the mail, check on staff, grab supplies. In and out. Not because I was terrified, but because I was convicted. Something about that building forced me to look in the mirror.

I wasn't scared of demons. I was scared of exposure.

Because I knew there were parts of me that weren't aligned. I knew there were things I hadn't surrendered. And how could I walk into a place and confront something evil if I hadn't yet confronted the darkness in me?

So I let it linger. Staff quit. Others stayed and told me about shadows in the hallway, voices, and terrorizing sleep paralysis at night. One woman said she saw figures watching her from the corner of the kennels. Another admitted she practiced witchcraft but told me not to worry—"I can handle it, boss."

That's when I realized this wasn't the 1980s church bubble anymore. Spirituality wasn't a Sunday thing—it had gone mainstream. Witchcraft was trending. People were burning sage and buying crystals like coffee.

And somewhere in the middle of it all, I realized maybe God wasn't punishing me.

He was answering me.

Not the prayers I posted about, but the ones I never said out loud. The ones buried under pride and disappointment.

For years I'd whispered it deep down where no one could hear—"God, if you're real…show me."

And He did.

Just not how I expected.

He didn't show me a miracle in the clouds or a goosebump moment at an altar call. He showed me that there was real evil. That the unseen wasn't imaginary. That the enemy didn't just live in horror movies; sometimes he rented buildings on prime real estate.

So, as I read Scripture again—almost embarrassed to even open that Bible after so long—I stumbled on something I hadn't read since I was nine years old. The first message I ever preached: from Ephesians 6.

Here the apostle Paul is writing a letter to individuals who seem to have been dealing with their own spiritual warfare. Paul's letter to the Ephesians hit different this time. I wasn't a kid rehearsing verses in a youth room. I was a man who had seen things I couldn't explain. When Paul wrote, "For we wrestle not against flesh and blood…" that word wrestle hit me in the gut.

> "For we wrestle not against flesh and blood, but against principalities, against powers, against the rulers of the darkness of this world, against spiritual wickedness in high places" (Ephesians 6:12 KJV).

Wrestle.

That's not a clean fight. That's face-to-face, hands locked, sweat, and pressure. You can't keep distance when you wrestle—you've got to engage.

And I realized that for years, I had avoided the fight.

I felt like I'd been slammed against the mat—pinned flat, lungs burning, staring up at the ceiling with no ref, no help, no way out.

I didn't even know if I was allowed to fight back.

And I sure as heck didn't know I could reach out my hand…and tag in my Partner.

For those of you who grew up in the '80s—or maybe still sneak in a little wrestling on TV—you know what I'm talking about. I'm not talking Olympic wrestling; I'm talking entertainment wrestling. Hulk Hogan. "Macho Man" Randy Savage. The Rock.

Those tag-team matches where one fighter's getting pummeled, running out of gas, seconds from losing the match—

and just when the crowd thinks it's over,

he stretches his hand across the mat,
barely touches his teammate's palm—
and the whole arena erupts.
Suddenly the man who was down is off the hook.
Fresh strength enters the ring.
Momentum shifts. The fight flips.
Looking back now, I think that's what was really happening to me.

Just like Jeff needed someone to step into that hallway back in Chapter 4, I didn't realize Someone had been standing ringside this whole time—hand out, waiting.

Someone who's never lost a battle.

Someone whose name makes hell tremble.

And when that revelation hit, a holy anger rose up inside me.

Why was I hesitating to go back into that building?

Why was I afraid to speak to that hallway—to bless what God had given me,

to cancel whatever dark contract had been written over that place?

Because the truth was—I wouldn't be walking in alone.

Paul said to put on the whole armor of God. The shield of faith. The sword of the Spirit—the Word of God. And for the first time in years, I believed it wasn't metaphor. It was strategy.

Because what was happening in that building wasn't just bad luck or coincidence—it was a war.

And I was being drafted back into it.

I decided to stop begging God to fix what He'd already given me authority over. I realized Jesus didn't just die to save me from something—He rose to empower me for something.

He looked at His disciples and said, "All authority has been given to Me in heaven and on earth" (Matthew 28:18 NKJV). And then He handed it over—keys to the Kingdom. Then He said, "I have given you authority to trample on snakes and scorpions and to overcome all the power of the enemy; nothing will harm you" (Luke 10:19 NIV). Authority over all the power of the enemy. Not some. All.

And that wrecked me.

Because it meant that the next time I stepped into a hallway like that—spirit or no spirit—I wouldn't be walking in as a victim or a skeptic. I'd be walking in as a son.

Maybe that building was never meant to be a pet spa. Maybe it was an altar. A collision zone. A place where heaven waited for someone to stop running and finally take a stand.

I stopped seeing this deal gone bad as a loss and started seeing it as a clue.

Because every time I prayed, every verse I read, every sleepless night that followed led me here—to the realization that this whole story wasn't about a haunted building at all.

It was about an unclaimed inheritance.

An authority that had been given but not used.

A war I was born to fight, but too distracted to engage.

And so, when I say this investigation didn't start with a headline or a tragedy—it started there.

At a locked door.

At a failed business.

At a haunted hallway.

It started the moment I realized I'd been standing at the threshold of something bigger all along.

Because that day, in Boca Raton, I thought I was walking into my next chapter in business—but what I really stepped into was the start of a deeper investigation.

A mirror.

A confrontation with everything I thought distance had buried.

That building wasn't the end of a dream; it was the beginning of an awakening. The moment that forced me to stop running from what I couldn't explain, and start asking the questions I'd spent my life avoiding.

Looking back, that story didn't have the happy ending I would've scripted. The business never reopened. The building was eventually shut down, and the project dissolved before I could make sense of what 91 had happened. By the time I realized who I was and the authority I carried, it was too late to run back and reclaim it. But that loss became a lesson. What I thought was failure turned out to be training—far more valuable than any million-dollar pet spa. God used that haunting to teach me where real authority begins.

And where this investigation led me next—the place where all the mystery, the dots, and the patterns finally converged—

was to a place I never planned to go.

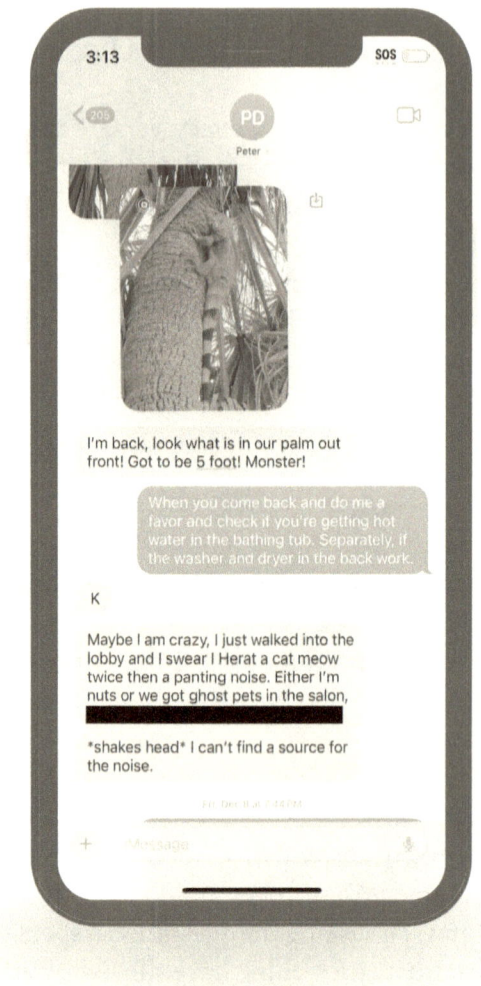

If you had received this message from your own employee, what would you have done?

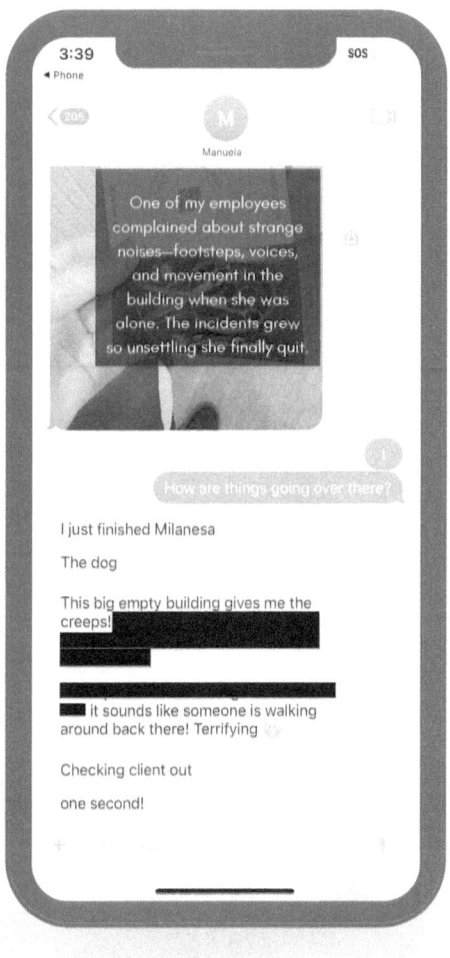

One of my employees complained about strange noises—footsteps, voices, and movement in the building when she was alone. The incidents grew so unsettling she finally quit.

How are things going over there?

I just finished Milanesa

The dog

This big empty building gives me the creeps!

it sounds like someone is walking around back there! Terrifying

Checking client out

one second!

Multiple employees. The same building. The same reports.
Coincidence… or a pattern?

I was trying to run a business. I wasn't looking for anything like this.

6

THE GATES
OF HELL

The Story They Hijacked

The devil doesn't need to destroy the Church He just needs to divide it.

I magine you stayed up late last night.

The campfire's still burning low—a faint hiss from a piece of wood curling smoke toward a sky full of stars. Peter's still talking—of course he is—arguing about whose turn it is to fetch water. We're laughing around the fire. We've been playing games for hours.

Jesus was known to carve little board games out of wood and bring them for game night. Andrew tried to keep score. John kept staring into the flames like he saw whole galaxies inside them.

Jesus laughed, too—real, unguarded—the kind of laugh that disarms you because you realize Heaven has a sense of humor.

We spent the last hour talking about the mysteries of the universe—questions that felt too heavy for the night air, but somehow, He made them sound simple.

By the time you finally drift toward sleep, you see the embers of the fire glowing. You take a deep breath, feeling that comfort—the kind that hits when you realize you're camping under the stars with the Creator of the universe.

A few minutes of deep rest, then—

a hand on your shoulder.

At first, you think it's Peter again, trying to steal the blanket. But then you hear that voice—calm and certain even at 3:30 a.m.

"Get up. We're going for a walk."

You blink. "Now?"

He smiles like He's already ten steps ahead.

"Now."

He's been up since before the stars began to fade—His usual hours. They say He prays between three and five every morning.

We've all wondered what He does up there on the mountain, but whatever it is, when He comes down, He's a man on a mission.

And here He is again—eyes bright, cloak still damp with dew, ready for the trip.

You grab your sandals, still half-dreaming, wondering where this road leads.

The others wake one by one—Thomas groaning, James muttering about the cold, Matthew clutching his ledger like he's trying to document every single thing we see.

The fire is only embers now. You step over them, out into the dark.

The air bites.

Your breath shows.

The first bird hasn't even thought about singing yet.

"Where are we going?" someone asks.

He doesn't answer—just starts walking north.

At first, you think He's headed back toward Galilee—maybe Capernaum—somewhere familiar, where news of His miracles spread like the daily headlines. But after a while, the landmarks change. The road narrows, twisting through rough hills—the kind of terrain soldiers use for shortcuts and thieves use for hiding.

Twenty-five miles.

Uphill.

Each step heavier than the last.

The sun claws its way over the horizon, turning the stones gold.

Sweat mixes with dust.

Your legs ache, but He keeps going—steady, purposeful—like He knows something you don't.

Hebrew fades from the road signs into Greek. Shrines appear where synagogues used to be. The smell of incense replaces the scent of baked bread. Every sense sharpens.

The disciples start whispering.

This isn't home territory anymore.

We're outside the safe zone.

Enemy territory.

You taste metal in the air—iron, like blood. The wind carries distant music—something dark, off-beat. A line of marble statues catches the light—half human, half beast.

And that's when it hits you—

He's leading you into their city.

Caesarea Philippi.

The place mothers warn their sons about.

Where idols drink blood and fear has an address.

Based on the warnings we'd heard growing up, this was one of the most demonic and haunted areas in the entire region. No rabbi in his right mind would walk this road.

But Jesus does.

And you follow—heartbeat loud in your ears—until the cliff appears, towering, scarred, water spilling from a cave so black it swallows the sun.

The locals call it the Gates of Hades—aka the gates of hell.

He stops.

Turns.

Scans the crowd.

And the air itself seems to hold its breath.

Then it happens…

With a sense of urgency on His face—not the same laughter from the night before when we played board games by the fire—the disciples can see it immediately: Jesus means business.

He starts with a question.

Almost like He tunes out the locals coming and going, arms full of incense and sacrifices for their idols.

Like He blocks out the witch doctors chanting their spells, yet without missing a beat of His own rhythm.

Confident.

Composed.

Like someone who owns the stage.

The question drops into the air.

"Who do they say I am?"

You think to yourself…Really?

Jesus, you're really bringing us to the doorstep of hell to have a Bible study?

But then you see His face—serious, focused, unchanging. He's waiting for an answer.

His eyes … piercing.

They don't just look at you; they read you.

It's like He can see your whole story, the parts you don't say out loud.

One disciple clears his throat.

The others shift, nervous, glancing around at the onlookers in their ritual robes.

"Some say you're John the Baptist…" someone offers.

Another adds, "Elijah."

A third mutters, "Maybe Jeremiah—or one of the prophets."

Their voices trail off into the echo of the spring.

But then Peter steps forward. For a second, you think he's about to say something reckless again. He always does. Yet this time his voice is steady…almost reverent.

He looks straight at Jesus and says, "You are the Christ

(the Messiah, the Anointed),

the Son of the living God" (Matthew 16:16 AMP).

Silence.

The kind that feels alive.

Jesus stares back at Peter for a long moment. A smile cracks across His face—the kind that says, Finally.

Approval.

Affection.

Recognition.

And then it lands hard…the most powerful spiritual flex and revelation in human history.

Pause.

That night around the fire dissolves—the warmth, the laughter, the glow—and what remains is that echo on the cliff. The laughter fades, but the revelation still burns.

This scene we've imagined—

was not fake.

It was real.

But for too long, based on my investigation, history—and maybe even evil itself—has gone out of its way to dilute the story.

To twist the truth.

To bury one of the most empowering moments ever given to people of faith.

As an investigator, I'm going to lay out the case.

You decide.

The story is recorded in the book of Matthew 16:13–18. His account flows with the most precision—capturing both the question and the revelation.

"When Jesus came into the region of Caesarea Philippi, He asked His disciples, saying, 'Who do men say that I, the Son of Man, am?'" (verse 13 NKJV).

And yes—that region was real. Literally real.

Now let's give a little historical account.

Excavations show that during Jesus's time, the Temple of Pan and Augustus had already been built by Herod the Great in 19 BC. The main spring—a cave mouth that gushed water from Mount Hermon—was called the Grotto of Pan (the Greek Paneion).

Pilgrims entered the city through a colonnaded road that led directly toward that cave. It was the literal heart of the city.

So when Matthew records that Jesus came "into the region of Caesarea Philippi" (verse 13 NKJV), the cultural and visual landmark everyone immediately pictured was that cave.

The gates.

The cliff.

The echoing spring.

And if you want more proof that this is where it all happened, just listen to His next words.

"The gates of hell shall not prevail against it" (verse 18 ESV).

That wasn't metaphor.

That was topography.

So imagine it this way.

It's Wednesday night. Your pastor says, "Bible study tonight," and then drives you out to one of the most haunted, paranormally charged places on Earth—right next to a graveyard where thousands were murdered to worship demon gods...

Does that set the picture?

That's what this was.

And if you know anything about Jesus—even from the moment He was twelve—you already know He doesn't wander anywhere by accident.

When His mother Mary lost Him in Jerusalem and finally found Him debating with the scholars and priests in the synagogue, He looked up and said, "I must be about My Father's business" (Luke 2:49 NKJV).

Yeah—that Jesus.

The same one who made blind eyes see and storms obey, just led His disciples to the gates of hell for a staff meeting.

He didn't make a move without it being intentional.

So let's dig deeper. Because there are clues in this chapter that will soon connect to names you've already seen in this book—and to names still coming.

Clues that tie to Charlie Kirk himself. And others that reach beyond headlines, beyond politics, into something eternal.

The implications here will speak to the skeptic, the critic, and the believer alike.

Yeah.

What happens next connects to all of us.

Jesus looks straight at Peter. The wind moves through the cliffs, whistling like breath through stone.

Then He speaks—the words that made the earth tremble and eternity lean in.

> "You are Peter (Petros in Greek)…and upon this rock I will build My Church." —Matthew 16:18 NKJV

Let's put our thumb on that for a second.

The word *Church*—ekklesia—didn't mean pews and stained glass. In the ancient world it meant a governing body, a civic assembly that carried legal authority to decide what would be permitted and what would be prohibited.

That same undertone flows straight into the New Testament.

So, what was Jesus doing here?

Was He founding a religion or authorizing a supernatural government under heaven's jurisdiction?

And then, as the disciples stand on that rocky ledge—hell literally rumbling beneath their feet—He adds the line that gave hell heartburn:

"And the gates of hell will not prevail against it [My Church]" (verse 18 NKJV).

Gates.

Not swords.

Not missiles.

Gates—defensive architecture.

Which means the Church was never meant to hide behind walls; it was designed to break them down.

Jesus wasn't giving us permission to play defense. He was handing us a warrant to invade. To kick in the gates and reclaim what hell has been hoarding—souls, purpose, peace, authority.

But that's not what most of us have seen.

Scroll social media and you'll hear it—

"Pray for me, the devil's been attacking me."

We sound cornered.

Pinned to the ropes, hoping to survive the next round.

Was that really His intention that morning?

To raise an army of beggars instead of warriors?

If so, this would've been the most anticlimactic crescendo in history—like a DJ building the track for five minutes, tension peaking, the crowd ready for the musical drop—and then someone yanks the power cord.

Because here's the deal:

I once heard Charlie Kirk say something that hit me like prophecy disguised as commentary:

"If pastors did their job, I'd be out of one."

Whether you were a fan or a critic, you can't deny that. | 103

He reached campuses the Church abandoned.

He provoked young minds in a generation allergic to conviction.

And maybe—just maybe—he said out loud what heaven has been whispering for years:

that the pulpits got comfortable while hell kept recruiting.

Drive through any city and you'll see it. Thirty churches in a five-mile radius, each one flying a different flag, each convinced it's holding the master key, and most of them quietly losing their children to boredom, hypocrisy, or both.

Maybe that's why Jesus didn't drop this revelation inside of church walls.

He walked twenty-five miles north, into enemy territory, and detonated truth where devils lived rent-free.

He wanted the ekklesia to know its job description:

To advance, not hide.

Now, about those post-event power grabs.

For centuries, theologians have argued over ownership of this moment.

Catholics claim it was the coronation of Peter—the first pope, the divine line of succession. Protestants counter that the Greek text tells another story. For readers who didn't major in Greek: the language uses gendered endings—one masculine, one feminine.

That small difference has fueled centuries of debate about what, exactly, Jesus meant. They point out that Jesus used two different words in that sentence—first calling Peter Petros (in the masculine, meaning "a small stone"), then shifting to petra (in the feminine, meaning "a massive rock formation").

So theologians have argued for centuries: Was Jesus building His Church on Peter the man, or on the revelation Peter had just spoken?

One was mortal.

The other, eternal.

And the debate keeps echoing: was Christ handing the keys to a single office—or unlocking access for every believer who would confess His name?

History shows what happens when men start drafting heaven's charter into bylaws. In medieval Europe, indulgences were sold like dollar-menu items—

Forgiveness for adultery: 9 coins.

Murder: 30.

It was religion's first paywall.

But before Protestants get too smug, let's admit our side-hustles. I've sat in arenas where preachers promised "prophetic upgrades" for a $1000 seed. I've watched a woman next to me whisper, 'Lord, I sold my car to get here…I can't buy a prayer.'

Different century, same spirit.

Whether it's incense or microphones, if it monetizes mercy, it misses the gospel.

If we are all the Body of Christ and the children of God—Heaven won't have a special section for Catholics and another for Evangelical Christians.

Because the real issue isn't robes or skinny jeans—it's men.

And the Bible gives us the number that tags every man-made system: six.

Created on the sixth day.

Branded on the beast.

666—the number of man.

So maybe what's been hijacking the Church isn't a denomination but an infection—pride dressed as priesthood. Systems built to insert middlemen between children and their heavenly Father.

Which brings us back to the logic of Heaven.

Would Jesus really rebuild the world on one man, when it was one man's pride that fractured it in Eden?

Would the second Adam hand creation's keys back to another Adam?

Unlikely.

What the enemy meant to weaponize, God flipped into revelation—and with one confession—You are the Christ—He multiplied it until hell's foundation shook.

And then history adds the twist nobody saw coming—

another man, not even at the scene—a persecutor-of-Christians-turned-fireball apostle named Paul, who would go on to write most of the New Testament.

That alone proves heaven doesn't play favorites.

It plays revelation.

If Peter's revelation opened the door, by God's grace—Paul built the hallway. And both men—flawed, forgiven—proved the same point: authority isn't inherited through robes or microphones. It's received through revelation.

So here's the question that lands like a gavel:

Who gains the most from convincing common everyday believers they have no authority?

Hell does.

That's the real hijacker.
The spirit that whispers, You're powerless.
The bureaucracy that builds ladders where Christ tore veils.
But the truth is louder:
You already carry the keys.
You already have the access.
And the only gate left to kick down is the one inside your own mind that says you can't.

From that rocky cliff in Caesarea Philippi to the far corners of the world, the pattern never changed. Every age faces its own gates—some carved in stone, others fortified by ideas. And in each generation, freedom demands invasion.

Historically, when it comes to good versus evil—stepping into enemy territory and tearing down fortified strongholds—no moment in modern history has captured it more vividly than that great day on the beaches of Normandy, June 6, 1944.

Evil incarnate had a name: Hitler.

His Nazi regime was marching across Europe, seizing nations, silencing dissent, and exterminating millions in gas chambers while the world held its breath.

That morning became known as D-Day—the largest amphibious invasion in human history.

And at the center of it all stood the United States of America, a nation founded on the belief that it was one nation under God, indivisible, with liberty and justice for all.

106 | When tyranny rose like a tide in Europe, America didn't wait for evil to knock on its shores.

It crossed the ocean.

It answered the call.

Because freedom, by nature, is not reactive—it's redemptive.

From England's coast, over 5,000 ships set sail, carrying nearly 160,000 men. Among them were the US Army Rangers and the 1st and 29th Infantry Divisions, headed for Utah and Omaha Beaches—the bloodiest and most decisive fronts of the entire invasion.

Machine-gun fire rained down as the landing craft opened.

Bodies fell.

Sand turned red.

But they advanced anyway.

Because the order had already been signed. The mission had already been authorized.

Failure was not an option.

By the end of that single day, American troops had broken through Hitler's so-called Atlantic Wall, punching a hole in what the Nazis swore was impenetrable. That breach opened the path to Paris, to Berlin, and ultimately—to victory.

The gates of tyranny fell.

And freedom marched in.

D-Day wasn't just a battle—it was a prophecy in motion.

Because what those soldiers did on the shores of Normandy is the same thing the Church was commissioned to do on the shores of history:

Invade enemy territory, tear down gates, and liberate captives.

And just like those soldiers weren't told to wait for Hitler to strike first, believers were never told to sit back and hope darkness tires itself out.

They were told to move forward—to storm the enemy's territory.

That same spirit of invasion—of righteous defiance—was first declared not in France, but in the backdrop of Caesarea Philippi, when Jesus turned to Peter and said, "On this rock I will build my church, and the gates of hell shall not prevail against it" (Matthew 16:18 ESV).

That was the original D-Day—the moment Heaven signed the legal warrant.

And the command was clear: Advance. Invade. Liberate.

So whether you're a believer or skeptic, a fan or a critic, the implications are real.

If Christ truly established a governing body meant to execute heaven's search-and-seizure mission on hell's territory—meant to reclaim what was stolen and push back darkness—then this affects every one of us.

It affects our families.

Our cities.

Our schools.

Our timelines.

Because if that body—the Church—is asleep, distracted, or confused…

If it's seduced by man-made systems and political theater…

If it's forgotten its badge of authority and settled for survival mode…

Then when the world calls for backup—

when evil seems to trend faster than truth—

there's a chance no one will answer the emergency call.

And maybe that's what hell has been counting on all along.

I can almost imagine hell's headquarters lighting up like a command center.

A red siren blaring.

A push notification on every demon's device: "The gates of hell will not prevail."

And in panic, they rush to rewrite the narrative—to make the Church believe those weren't marching orders, but a memo to retreat.

Confuse the Church, and you can hijack a nation.

That's always been hell's playbook—confusion before conquest. Seduce it with comfort, and you can stall revival. Convince it that prayer is paperwork and authority is arrogance—and you've just hijacked heaven's embassy.

So maybe the question isn't whether the gates of hell will prevail.

Maybe the question is—who left them locked?

Because Heaven already handed over the keys.

And you already have the badge.

And this world doesn't need more spectators—it needs a Church that remembers it was built to storm gates.

Fittingly, this is Chapter 6—the number of man.

Maybe that's the point.

This story—the moment Jesus handed down marching orders to His Church—wasn't just corrupted by devils; it was rewritten by man-made doctrines.

But grace always leaves a paper trail.

Even as the case file seems closed, the evidence keeps whispering. Some patterns refuse to stay buried. They rise through names and places—like divine fingerprints on history's case file.

It's worth noting that throughout this investigation, I discovered something almost prophetic.

Charlie Kirk was shot in Orem, Utah.

The very name Kirk—Charlie's last name—literally means church in its original Scottish and Old Norse roots.

So when we say "Kirk means church," that isn't just poetic—it's etymology.

But there's another layer—one buried in the Hebrew. The word Orem (עָרֵם —Strong's 6193) translates as craftiness or shrewdness—the same root used in Genesis 3:1 NIV, where it says:

"Now the serpent was more crafty than any of the wild animals which the Lord God had made."

That Hebrew root ('-r-m) threads straight through Scripture, marking the defining trait of the deceiver himself.

So while the city of Orem wasn't named for that word, the linguistic echo is undeniable. While the city's modern name has its own origin and history, one can't help but notice a chilling parallel in the ancient Hebrew root—a word that once described the serpent's craftiness in Eden. Whether coincidence or providence, the echo is hard to ignore: its very syllables seem to whisper the shadow of the crafty one.

Some would call it coincidence. Others would call it a pattern hiding in plain sight. Because in the same way Kirk means church, Orem, by its Hebrew mirror, points back to craftiness—to the serpent's intelligence, the dragon's deceit. And when you line them side by side, the translation reads almost like prophecy:

The Church was shot by the crafty one.

The Church was struck by the dragon.

And as any good investigator knows—when you're tracing the aftermath of an attack, definitions matter.

To hijack means to seize control of something already in motion—an aircraft, a vehicle, a system—and reroute it toward a destination it was never meant to reach. It doesn't destroy the vessel outright; it just quietly redirects it.

That's the danger.

And whether you're a fan or a critic, you've probably felt that word before.

Moments when your dream was hijacked.

Your purpose hijacked.

A relationship that detoured off the map—leaving you wondering if it was God steering the wheel or something darker rerouting you mid-flight.

We've all been there.

We've all felt the stall.

The quiet drift away from where we thought we were headed.

So pause and ask yourself—if the enemy's tactic is rerouting, where in your life did he change your coordinates? Where did your joy get delayed? Where did the mission lose altitude?

Why would God go through all the trouble to incorporate and establish His Church on the earth—to sign it into legal existence as Heaven's governing body—only for it to forget where it's going?

The takeaway:

The evidence points to one six-letter word sitting at the center of this entire controversy—Church.

That's the headline.

That's the pattern.

Every clue, every theological detour, every debate about power, hierarchy, or silence circles back to that single word.

It's not coincidence that Kirk means church.

That clue belongs on the evidence board too. Because the very name tied to this tragedy echoes the condition of the modern body of Christ—divided, distracted, still arguing over who holds the keys instead of storming the gates together.

So maybe the dragon never needed open warfare.

Maybe all he ever needed was a divided Church.

And that's the six-letter word that changes everything.

Church.

The case file points to it.

The cross paid for it.

And heaven is still waiting for its governing body to remember who it is.

The gates were never meant to keep you out—they
were meant to prove you could kick them down.

And maybe that's the connection.

Because as I pin the Church itself to my evidence board—the Bride, the Body, the only entity on Earth given authority to invade hell's gates—the red string points to a chilling question.

The last forty-eight hours of Charlie's life weren't just political—they were spiritual. Every credible account points to a family battling unseen warfare.

Etsy curses.

Fear in the night.

A priest called the night before.

That's not speculation; that's part of the record. It shows how real the conflict was.

And as I trace that line across the map of this investigation, I can't help but ask…

What would've happened if the Church—capital C—had sounded the alarm?

If believers across America had prayed in agreement instead of arguing online?

If pastors who quoted him from their pulpits had taken up arms in the Spirit instead of debating whether they agreed with his politics?

Would Charlie have survived?

And while we're on the subject—it's not the first time a nation stood at a spiritual crossroads.

What would've happened if Jesus Christ Himself, or the Apostle Paul carrying His Spirit, had walked into the White House during the final weeks of Abraham Lincoln's life—when séances were being held in the East Room to contact the dead?

Would destiny have shifted if someone carrying the living Christ had spoken life into that room?

And while we're at it—how many tragedies in history might trace[111] back not to the wrath of God, but to the silence of His people? Could it be that we—the Body—bear some responsibility?

I know that's a hard pill to swallow. But every investigator knows you don't close a case until you've questioned every possible suspect.

And that includes us.

Because maybe…just maybe…the Church was too quick to sanitize the story.

Too eager to call Charlie a martyr before asking if he could have been a miracle.

Was that language—martyr—a badge of honor…or a cover story to excuse our own ineffectiveness?

Did we proclaim him fallen so we wouldn't have to face the possibility that we failed to stand?

I'm not accusing.

I'm asking.

Because when the Bride goes silent, evil fills the vacancy. And if the serpent's final strategy was to fracture the Church—to make us debate each other instead of defending one another—then maybe the real crime scene isn't just in Orem, Utah. It's in every sanctuary where unity turned into apathy and authority turned into showmanship.

Maybe that's why Jesus prayed, on the eve of His own murder, that we would be one. Jesus didn't just pray for the lost, or for His own endurance, but for us?

He looked up toward heaven and said:

"I do not pray for these alone, but also for those who will believe in Me through their word; that they all may be one, as You, Father, are in Me, and I in You; that they also may be one in Us, that the world may believe that You sent Me." —John 17:20–21 NKJV

> The final battle of the end times might not begin with beasts or wars, but with the fracturing of the Bride—believers who stop fighting the gates of hell because they're too busy fighting each other.

And maybe that's why, in the next chapter, we'll open a new case file—one that asks a harder, more dangerous question:

What if Charlie—and others—didn't have to die?

7

THE MARTYR WE MISSED

Was It a Cover-Up?

The moment the world turned key witnesses into tragic headlines.

It was a cold Monday morning near St. Louis, Missouri.

Three boys were off school for the Martin Luther King Jr. holiday—no classes, no homework, just open time and a frozen lake that looked safe enough to explore.

They decided to head out and enjoy the outdoors, unaware of the danger waiting for them. As publicly reported by multiple news outlets, including FOX 11, fourteen-year-old John Smith and his two friends had recently won a basketball game and were still buzzing from the victory. They walked toward Lake Sainte Louise, laughing and full of energy—just boys celebrating a day off school, their breath visible in the winter air.

Then came the sound. A single crack. Then another.

The laughter stopped.

The ice gave way.

All three plunged into the forty-degree water—fifteen feet deep, black, silent. Two of the boys managed to pull themselves out with the help of neighbors who heard the screams. John disappeared beneath the ice.

At 11:31 a.m., a 911 call came through. Firefighters arrived roughly twenty minutes later. During those long minutes John was still under the surface. Diver Tommy Shine later said he heard an inner voice whisper, Go back one more time. He did—and saw a sleeve drift by. He pulled.

John had been unlucky enough to be submerged in the freezing water for a full fifteen minutes before EMTs were able to reach him and transport his lifeless body to the nearby St. Joseph Hospital West, where life-saving measures were underway.

No pulse. No breath. Skin blue. They started CPR right there on the bank. When the ambulance finally reached the hospital, John had been without a heartbeat for forty-three minutes.

Inside the ER, Dr. Kent Sutterer led the resuscitation team. They worked relentlessly. Chest compressions. Epinephrine. Oxygen. Nothing. Flatline.

By the time his mother got there—running through the hallways, praying under her breath—she was told the words no parent ever wants to hear: "There's nothing more we can do."

But there was something different about this moment. She wasn't going to be denied. No—not when her son's life was on the line.

A woman of deep and abiding faith, she entered John's room, "walked up to the end of the bed and felt his feet, how cold and gray they were," as she later recalled to local news outlets, and began to pray— loudly. "I remembered in church all my life hearing this Scripture that says, 'The Holy Spirit who raised Christ Jesus from the dead,'" as she further recalled. "I thought to myself, 'You're either who You say You are or You're not.' The minute I prayed, 'Holy Spirit, please come and give me back my son!' his heartbeat started."

Within weeks he walked out of that hospital against all odds. This true story was later turned into a movie titled *Breakthrough*.

Dr. Kent Sutterer later said there was no medical explanation for what he witnessed.

This mom refused to let her son's story end in tragedy.

She refused to let this become a missed moment.

And it made me wonder—
what if she had?
What if she'd accepted the verdict, bowed to the noise, walked away?
How does heaven look at moments like that—

the ones that could have ended differently if someone had only stepped in, spoken up, believed again?

Let me take you to a mountaintop.

One of the most breathtaking views on earth. Jesus stood on the ridge above the city, olive branches shifting in the wind. The sun caught the Temple walls like fire, and below, Jerusalem buzzed with the sound of Passover—laughter, animals, footsteps, life. But Heaven was quiet. He saw it all, and He wept.

One of only three moments Scripture ever shows us the Creator of the universe in tears.

And instead of laughing by a campfire with His disciples, telling stories, or giving authority at the gates of hell—this time, He's weeping.

You might ask yourself, why did Jesus weep?

From what the text tells us, He was weeping because of missed opportunities.

It was just days before His arrest. The cross was already casting its shadow. And yet His tears weren't for Himself—they were for the people who could've known peace but didn't.

Let's look at what the text actually says:

"As He approached Jerusalem and saw the city, He wept over it and said, 'If you, even you, had only known on this day what would bring you peace—but now it is hidden from your eyes… because you did not recognize the time of God's coming to you.'" —Luke 19:41–44 NIV

This scene reveals something astonishing:

The heart of God can break over missed moments.

They had a chance to recognize Him as the Messiah. He says it plainly—if they'd only known, it would have brought them peace. But instead, they walked into their own destruction, and He could already see what was coming.

And to God, it wasn't, Oh well. You made your choice.

It wasn't, You made your bed, now lie in it. |117

To God, it was tragic.

It was personal.

It brought Him to tears.

And I can't help but wonder—
how many times have we done the same?
How many moments have passed us by—

moments when the Prince of Peace was near,
but we didn't recognize Him?

What I'm about to say next may make you uncomfortable, but sometimes families need to have uncomfortable conversations. The kind you have around the kitchen table. Like the intimate moments after a funeral. The kind where the final will and testament is on the table, and everyone's forced to talk about what's been avoided.

I know that table well.

To give you some context—by trade, I run an estate-sale company. Not glamorous. Not flashy. It's the world of handling what's left after someone dies. But it puts me in rooms most people never see—rooms frozen in time right after loss.

The couch still holds their shape.

The coffee's still in the cabinet.

The air still smells like them.

And the family stands there, quiet, trying to figure out what to do next.

They call us to handle the stuff. We tag the dishes, the records, the jewelry. We open the doors. Strangers walk through someone's life, holding memories and saying, "Ten bucks?" And just like that—a lifetime gets liquidated.

It's sacred and savage all at once.

Because in those moments, you realize: you can't take it with you.

Pharaohs tried. Look how that ended—gold still in the tombs, bodies long gone.

But here's what I've learned after years of watching families sort through the remains: Grief always forces conversations—the kind we avoided when it mattered most.

That's what this chapter is.

A family conversation.
The kind we didn't plan to have.

Because when Charlie Kirk was assassinated, something cracked in the spirit. For good or bad, everyone felt it. And the word that started circling like smoke was *martyr*.

"Charlie was a martyr."

I heard it everywhere—in sermons, tweets, interviews.

And I get it. Martyr feels noble. It gives pain a frame.

But if we're not careful, it also helps us dodge the harder question:

Did Charlie have to die that day?

That's not accusation. It's a spiritual question…

Now, as I saw news interviews, podcasts, and even memorial services, I saw leader after leader, politician after politician, stand up and say, Charlie was a martyr just as Stephen from the New Testament.

Who was Stephen?

He was a man on fire—preaching about a God who no longer lived in buildings, but in people. That message lit up the early streets of Jerusalem and set the religious establishment on edge. The Sanhedrin, the most powerful council of the day, couldn't stand it. To them, it wasn't revelation; it was rebellion. They accused him of blasphemy, dragged him outside the city, and stoned him to death for daring to say that Heaven had moved in.

We meet him in Acts 6.

Bold. Brilliant. Full of faith. Performing miracles.

They throw rocks.

But before he dies, he looks up—and something wild happens.

He sees Heaven open.

Jesus, standing at the right hand of God.

Standing.

Now put your thumb on that…let's look deeper at the implications of what this Bible passage says.

Everywhere else, the Bible says Jesus is seated—seated in power, seated in authority.

But here He stands.

So by tradition, to explain this scene, Jesus is standing in Stephen's vision as he's dying.

Preachers say He stood to welcome Stephen home.

Maybe…

But what if Jesus was standing for a different reason?

See, from the time I was young, I was always the type to double-check the story.

If someone said the sky was blue, I'd ask, "How do you know?"

If they said, "Because it just is," I'd still step outside to see for myself.

So when I read about Jesus—this same Jesus who stopped funeral processions and interrupted death like it was trespassing—I had to ask the question nobody seemed to be asking.

Because it's hard to picture Him just standing there…smiling… waiting to welcome someone home—almost like a tragic murder was part of the plan.

Not this Jesus.

Not the one who had just commissioned His followers to heal the sick, cast out demons, and raise the dead.

Not the one who gave authority over all the power of the enemy.

So I asked myself—
what if He wasn't standing to applaud Stephen?

What if He was standing to step in?

What if Heaven was already leaning forward to intervene…

but no one on earth moved?

What if Heaven wanted the news headline to be "Miracle on Main Street" instead of "Tragic Death"?

Right after Stephen's death, persecution ignited.
Believers scattered.
The text doesn't say revival broke out.
It says they ran.
That wasn't momentum. That was survival.
So maybe the real question isn't, "Why did Stephen die?"

Maybe it's, "Did he have to?"

The Bible shows us what's possible when faith acts—and what happens when it doesn't. Scholars call it prescriptive versus descriptive text. Prescriptive tells you what God wants you to do. Descriptive just tells you what actually happened. Prescriptive would be: "Love your enemies." Descriptive? The disciples casting lots to fill Judas's seat—a pre–Holy Spirit coin toss over who gets the twelfth chair.

That's what makes the Bible credible—it doesn't Photoshop humanity out of the story. It gives us the raw unedited footage.

I started wondering if maybe what I'd been told all along wasn't the whole story.

I kept reading—that same book, Acts—the one that doesn't sanitize anything. It gives you the good, the bad, and the ugly of the Church's birth, its growing pains, and its early rough edges.

I decided to continue with my investigation.

So, as I pin this document to my evidence board, the next word—the next lead—was martyr.

Everything on the news felt so quick to sanitize and say, "Move on here…nothing to see," spiritually speaking.

I didn't know Charlie personally, and I have nothing to do with his organization. But we're part of the same faith family, so I thought it was wise to investigate this quick claim to categorize Charlie as a martyr just because he was murdered—while speaking. Because if we rush to call Charlie a martyr just to numb our guilt, we're not honoring him—we're excusing ourselves.

Some have quoted Tertullian, an early Church father, who said:

"The blood of the martyrs is the seed of the Church."

It's a striking line. And yes, many brave believers have given their lives for the gospel.

But if we're not careful, we turn that quote into a doctrine—one that quietly suggests the Church needs more blood to keep growing. That God needs martyrs to supplement His mission.

But that's not what Scripture says.

Hebrews 10:10 NIV is clear:

"We have been made holy through the sacrifice of the body of Jesus Christ once for all."

Once.

For all.

That means the only blood that needed to be spilled for the Church to be born was His.

We don't need more sacrifices.

We need hearts awakened by truth, not restrained by religion.

And if we're not careful, we start honoring Christian deaths more than we honor resurrection power.

We glorify loss—when we should be stopping it. That's not reverence. That's surrender dressed up as sanctity.

So, I continued to look for clues that would help me understand what *martyr* originally meant.

Then I found the verse that threw a spotlight on this controversial word.

It wasn't hidden in some obscure letter or buried in translation—it was right there in Jesus' final words before His ascension:

> "But you will receive power when the Holy Spirit comes on you; and you will be my witnesses in Jerusalem, and in all Judea and Samaria, and to the ends of the earth." —Acts 1:8 NIV

That word *witnesses* in Greek? *martyrs*.

The same root where we get the word *martyr*.

But Jesus wasn't sending them out to die. He was sending them out to live.

To fight.

To cast out darkness.

How could they war against evil if they were all meant to be taken out too early?

He was sending them out to testify—with power.

To speak.

To heal.

The early Church later turned that word into something else...
We turned witnesses into casualties.
We sanctified tragedy and called it revival.
But resurrection—His kingdom come, on earth as it is in Heaven—is supposed to be the story.
Not silence.

So yes, Charlie was a martyr—according to the biblical definition. A bold witness. But maybe the martyr we missed was the moment.

Now understand—I have respect for Charlie's boldness. I didn't have to agree with everything he said or how he said it. But someone who will debate others and even give them the mic first to lay out their case—that's admirable in a culture that refuses to hear points from the opposing side.

That's what sent me back to the beginning—to the birth of the Church.

Let's revisit that timeline, because what I uncovered might shock you. It might challenge everything you've been taught.

I grew up in church—literally playing with toy cars on the pews—hearing thousands of sermons.

And the deeper I dug, the more I realized how much we might have missed.

Luke, a physician by trade, is widely believed to have been the author of the book of Acts.

He gives us a crime scene of sorts.

"About that time Herod the king laid violent hands on some who belonged to the church" (Acts 12:1 ESV).

Does that headline sound familiar? "Violence against the church"?

The Church was on fire.

Christ had risen, handed them the keys of the Kingdom.

Peter preached a message; three thousand believed.

And then, as we've discovered, the first martyr after Christ's death and resurrection appeared—Stephen.

And just as people today use martyr, Stephen's story became the first of its kind.

So then I had to ask…this twisting of what the word originally meant—

Was it intentional?

Why and how did this word *martyr* get twisted from a person who boldly proclaims their faith—a witness—to now a victim…someone pre-subscribed for a funeral?

Who would want to change or dilute the original intent of the word from powerful witness for Christ to someone destined for an early death?

As I began to see traditions—handed down by people—I looked deeper into what was really happening for the early Church in the New Testament.

Soon after Stephen's murder, James, one of the original disciples, was arrested and killed. Luke, being as detailed as he was, never mentions in the book of Acts that anyone prayed for James. It just happened. No other details or clues. And then Luke jumps to a news report—telling readers that King Herod set his eyes on Peter next.

Now, being that Luke was a doctor by trade—detailed—why would he not give us a clue if it was important?

What was happening to the early New Testament Church behind the scenes?

Maybe the early Church was still learning what authority looked like. Just like when you buy the newest, hottest phone with all the apps—and you're not fully sure how to use it or all its powerful features.

Maybe the early Church missed it with Stephen. Maybe again with James.

But something shifted when Peter was arrested. Yes…this great leader Peter—the first to connect the dots and answer the question right when Christ was revealing Himself as the Son of God, the Messiah. That same man who preached with power and authority and three thousand people got saved days prior. Now Herod—the same Herod, in this context, that Luke says was violently targeting the Church—may have wanted to stoke more fear into early Christians and make an example out of Peter.

But then you see something suddenly change in the text.

The text says the Church prayed, and not with polite words.

Luke chooses the Greek word ἐκτενῶς (ektenōs)—to stretch out, to reach beyond normal strength, to pray as if life itself depends on it.

It's the same intensity Luke once used to describe Jesus praying in Gethsemane until His sweat became like blood.

Maybe the same type of ektenōs prayer Joyce Smith made in the E.R. for her son, John.

This wasn't a grace-before-dinner prayer at Thanksgiving. No.

This was warfare. This was a governing body taking authority and not wanting to have another missed martyr on their hands.

And Heaven responded.

Let's read the Scripture:

"It was about this time that King Herod arrested some who belonged to the church, intending to persecute them. He had James, the brother of John, put to death with the sword. When he saw that this met with approval among the Jews, he proceeded to seize Peter also… So Peter was kept in prison, but the church was earnestly praying to God for him."
—Acts 12:1–5 NIV

"The night before Herod was to bring him to trial, Peter was sleeping between two soldiers, bound with two chains, and sentries stood guard at the entrance. Suddenly an angel of the Lord appeared and a light shone in the cell. He struck Peter on the side and woke him up. 'Quick, get up!' he said, and the chains fell off Peter's wrists…Peter followed him out of the prison, but he had no idea that what the angel was doing was really happening; he thought he was seeing a vision."
—Acts 12:6–9 NIV

Chains fell. Doors opened. Peter walked free.
Divine intervention—through the prayers of ordinary people.
Read that again slowly.

Peter was in chains…

But the Church.

Herod had the power…

But the Church.

Soldiers surrounded him…

But the Church.

A public execution was on the calendar…

But the Church…prayed.

Let's pause there.

The Bible doesn't say the Church prayed earnestly for James.
Maybe they did. Maybe they didn't.
But this time—with Peter—they refused to miss another moment.
I wonder what it would feel like if a social media story went viral...
with a trending hashtag...

#ButTheChurch

So then what happened next—as the early Church began to wake
up to the authority Jesus gave them?
I'm glad you asked. Let's find out why.
It's important to read the very next verse in this biblical account.
Luke, the writer, keeps rolling into the next verse—no chapter break,
no time skip.
Now this next part—I'd never connected the dots, even though I
grew up in church.

The bad guy—Herod—most likely influenced by evil—went to
Caesarea. He basked in applause. He acted like a god.
And the same hand that freed Peter struck Herod down.

The Bible tells us the angel of the Lord struck him dead. Yes...
could we be looking at the first hit job in the New Testament?
Like the old mafia bosses ordering a hit on a rival gang?
The man who killed James was now eaten from within. The irony.
Let's look at the biblical account: "Immediately, because Herod
did not give praise to God, an angel of the Lord struck him down, and
he was eaten by worms and died" (Acts 12:23 NIV).

126| This news headline sent shockwaves throughout the ancient world.

Such a shock for the people of that time that even later, the non-
Christian, very well-respected historian Josephus confirmed this in
historical writings. One of those rare moments the Bible intersects
with independent historical accounts.
Josephus further states that while Herod was receiving this praise, "a
severe pain also arose in his belly, and began in a most violent manner."
He later explains that "he was carried into the palace, and the rumor
went abroad everywhere, that he would certainly die in a little time."

So how does the writer of Acts seem to know the reason the angel of the Lord killed Herod? Let's read what he says.

Basically, Luke writes that it happened because Herod did not give glory to God—in other words,

because he accepted divine worship from the people of Tyre and Sidon.

But how did Luke know?

Did he interview the angel over coffee?

Or was Heaven still answering the Church's prayer—finishing what had been started in that jail cell—one verse prior?

Could it be that the Church had finally discovered its voice?

As I'm putting this piece of evidence—the word *martyr*—on my evidence board, and looking at missed opportunities in the Church compared to moments the Church got it right…

Then…

the strangest thing happens.

After Acts 12, the miracles keep coming—until Acts 28—and then…nothing.

Paul raises Eutychus, survives shipwrecks, heals Publius's father on Malta—and the story ends mid-sentence.

No farewell. No closure.

Just silence.

And that silence started to feel intentional.

We're told the apostles died as martyrs, that the power died with them. But Scripture records no apostles' deaths after the book of Acts. Everything else? Second-hand testimony. Hearsay. If this were an investigation, any good detective would circle that in red.　　　| 127

Why were the most explosive years of the early Church cut off so abruptly?

Why does the record stop just when the fire was spreading?

Why do the legends that follow sound more like damage control than victory reports?

Which brings us back to Charlie, JFK, Lincoln, and others…

I searched every record I could find—interviews, livestreams, eyewitness statements. I didn't hear a single moment where someone—filled with the Spirit of God—stepped in and canceled darkness.

No one publicly rebuked death or spoke words of life.

Maybe it happened privately. I hope it did.

I heard people say, "There was nothing we could do."

That line haunts me.

Because Jesus once said to His disciples, "Heal the sick, raise the dead, …cast out demons" (Matthew 10:8 NKJV).

Not metaphor. Not suggestion. Command.

He said that before the cross.

Before the resurrection.

Before the Spirit came.

And if they had that much authority then, how much more do we have now?

So why is the Church so quiet when fear or death walks in?
We mourn. We post. We hashtag.

But Heaven waits for someone to speak.

And maybe that's the **cover-up.**
Not the one happening in the media.
The one happening in the spirit.
When a Church built for resurrection forgets how to use it.

Because if the good guys were really winning—if miracles were multiplying—why sanitize the story?

Why re-edit the war reports into tragedies?

Who benefits when a Church that once raised the dead and watched angels strike down tyrants starts accepting death as destiny?

Back to the first person Church tradition has told us to call a martyr—Stephen. He was preaching about the Holy Spirit living in humans and not temples made with hands—like cathedrals and buildings.

Do you understand how scandalous Stephen's viral social media post would be?

He suggested that *now* the God of the universe, the Spirit of Christ Himself, was not limited to buildings, but that He lived in everyday people.

The Church could lose its monopoly on God—so...they killed Stephen.

And then the word *martyr*—magically—got twisted.

As I continued to investigate, I wanted to see what Heaven thought about martyrs. I found this interesting passage.

When John recorded his vision in Revelation 6:9 saying that he "saw under the altar the souls of those who had been slain because of the word of God and the testimony they had maintained" (NIV), he wasn't glorifying death.

The Greek word there for *testimony* is *martyria*—the root of our word *martyr*. They were not martyrs because they died; they were martyrs because they testified, and because they would not be silenced, they were killed. Heaven honors their boldness, clothes them in white robes, and promises that justice will be done.

But nowhere does the passage say God willed their slaughter. Nowhere does it tell the Church to sit back and romanticize their blood as fuel for revival. In fact, the cry from beneath the altar is a cry for justice—"How long, O Lord?"—which tells us Heaven longs for an end to that kind of loss.

As I rerouted my attention to the early Church, the more I looked, the more it felt like a cover-up.

Not an accident. Something done by design.

Someone wanted the Church to believe the battle was over. It seemed that someone wanted the heroes remembered for their deaths, not their victories. Someone wanted the story to end at Acts 28— | 129 before the next chapter could ever be written.

And that brings us back to the woman in the St. Louis emergency room. She wasn't an apostle. She wasn't a theologian. But she stretched herself in that same ektenōs prayer.

And Heaven answered.

A pulse returned.

A miracle happened.

So who's right here?

Has Jesus been standing, waiting to intervene, while His Church sits convinced it no longer has authority?

Have we been too quick to post halos with hashtags and label every loss "God's timing"?

Because if Acts ends the way it does, it begs a question every detective learns to ask:

Who had something to gain by the twisting of a controversial word like *martyr*?

Who profits when a living, miracle-working Church stops believing it can still move mountains?

The deeper I dug, the stranger it got.

The book of Acts doesn't fade out like a memoir. It stops—mid-sentence, mid-miracle, mid-moment. No closing credits. No benediction. Just silence.

Most of the apostles—other than Paul—abruptly vanish. No word on their whereabouts. Nada. Zilch.

Why?

Why did the early Church romanticize this idea of martyrs and convince early Christians that being a witness for Christ meant dying too young—tragically—as if that somehow glorified God?

And that silence still echoes.

The investigation isn't over.

There's one last step at any crime scene once you've bagged the evidence, mapped the blood-spatter, traced every fingerprint.

You go to the morgue.

You perform the autopsy.

You open the silence to find out how they really died—hoping to uncover the real assassin.

And with that lingering question in mind…what if the martyrs we missed weren't just the ones who died?

What if they were the moments we buried—the witnesses we ignored, the testimonies we never told?

The conversations that could've healed.

The prayers that could've changed outcomes.

The faith that could've raised something back to life.

8

SPIRITUAL AUTOPSY

The Jezebel and Balaam Connection

Case File R 2:20
Wrong aisle. Wrong bed.

M ost of us know what it's like—to be cheated on, or to cheat.
The act is done.
Loyalty splits.

Secrets multiply.

It gets complicated fast.

Because what begins in bedrooms eventually bleeds into boardrooms, pulpits, and politics.
The private affair becomes a public pattern.
We live in a culture addicted to contradiction—

ideologies intermarrying,

convictions cross-pollinating,

truth and trend tangled in the same bed.

Just last week I met a man with two tattoos that didn't belong together—one a Scripture verse, the other an ancient symbol that meant the exact opposite.
He wore both proudly, unaware that his skin had become a sermon about our times:
a generation trying to mix light and darkness and call it balance.
Because to reach a verdict on where God is in all this chaos, we'll need to look through time itself—past, present, and what's still coming.
If God is eternal Spirit, He's not bound by the clock.

So we're going to do what every investigator dreams of doing: we're going back to the future.

We'll trace the pattern forward and backward until we find where He still stands—and where we left Him.

Because somewhere between history and heartbreak, the trail goes cold.

And that's where we pick it up.

I have friends on all sides.

Pastors and atheists.

Artists and analysts.

Believers, skeptics, and everyone in between.

I think it's important to sit down and break bread with people—even those you don't fully agree with.

It sharpens you.

It humbles you.

It helps you see the world from another angle.

Some of you reading this might be lifelong Michael Jackson fans. Others might admire JFK.

Maybe you were intrigued by Charlie Kirk, even if you'd never admit it out loud because his name could split a room in seconds.

Would it help if I told you that none of that matters? Who you like—or don't like—isn't the point. Because behind every headline, every celebrity, every trending post…the real question has always been the same:

Was God there when we needed Him, or wasn't He?

That's what we're tracing in this investigation—not the gossip, but the fingerprints.

The goal isn't to judge the victims; it's to understand the pattern.

To see whether by studying the past, we can discern where darkness plans to strike next.

And this is where the case blows wide open.

It's not easy to write a chapter like this.

> Not because the facts are unclear—
> but because the implications are serious.

We're not dissecting conspiracy theories or throwing stones at the grieving. We're pulling back the curtain on very public tragedies and asking sobering, spiritual questions most people are too afraid to voice out loud.

What actually happened in the final forty-eight hours of Charlie Kirk's life?

What was going on—spiritually—beneath the surface?

This isn't an accusation.

It's an investigation.

This isn't a hit piece.

It's a **spiritual autopsy**.

And before we begin, let me say this as clearly as possible: This is not a war against Catholics.

This isn't about which denomination is better.

This isn't about whose rituals are right.

Heaven isn't divided into sections. There's no Section A for Catholics and Section B for Evangelicals. There's just one family.

Even the thief who hung beside Jesus—a convicted criminal with who-knows-what kind of rap sheet—looked over and said, "Remember me when You enter Your kingdom."

And Jesus looked right back and said, "Today, you'll be with Me in Paradise."

(As recorded in Luke 23:42–43 NKJV.)

No doctrinal exams. Just desperation and trust.

So let's get that BIG PINK ELEPHANT out of the room now.

This is not Catholic vs. Protestant.

This is a wake-up call for the whole Church.

So what happened in those final hours—Let's start with what we know. | 137

THE LAST 48 HOURS

By now you already know the name at the heart of this investigation.

Jezebel.

The same magazine we've referenced in earlier chapters—the one that turned witchcraft into a headline—had already written itself into this story long before Charlie Kirk's final hours.

In September 2025, *Jezebel* ran what it called a "feature." The rest of the world recognized it for what it was: a hit piece.

And it wasn't political. It was spiritual. Openly so.

The article celebrated the idea that witches had been paid on Etsy to place curses on Charlie. We've traced these details before. But here, they take on new weight.

> For context: Etsy is an online marketplace where people usually sell handmade crafts, jewelry, and art.

This was no satire, no metaphor. It was the literal invocation of witchcraft—the same kind that, historically, has been used to intimidate prophets and dismantle kings.

Ironically, a century-and-a-half earlier, the same spirit appeared—only the setting was different. In Lincoln's day it was a séance in the Red Room; in ours, it was witchcraft for sale on Etsy. Different century, same darkness.

And something strange happened next.

Megyn Kelly, the influential media personality and close friend of the Kirk family, said publicly that both Charlie and his wife, Erika, read the article. They took it seriously. They were, in her words, "rattled."

And I have to pause here.

Because I watched how quickly some pastors brushed this off—not because they had the facts, but because they didn't like the man.

Ask yourself: how far have we fallen when spiritual gatekeepers are willing to tolerate witchcraft simply because they disagree with the victim?

When did discernment become optional, and bitterness become theology?

It's like a shepherd who spots a wolf circling the neighboring 138 | flock—tearing through the sheep—but shrugs it off because he doesn't like that breed of sheep anyway.

The wolf doesn't care whose pasture it starts in.

It always comes for the next gate.

Back to Charlie:

In response, they called a Catholic priest—a family friend—to come and pray over Charlie that very night.

Let that timeline sink in.

Curses declared.

Fear found a crack.

A priest was called.

And within 24 hours…Charlie Kirk was gone.

No one can claim to know the exact link between those events—only God knows that. But the timing compels us to look deeper at how fear can open doors in any of our lives.

Now pause with me.

Because I'm not here to point fingers at anyone.

I'm not here to mock Catholic rituals.

I'm not here to say what was prayed or wasn't.

We don't know. Only God does.

But what I am here to do is raise the questions that nobody else seems to be asking:

- Why did this family feel the need to call in a spiritual professional?
- What was said in those final prayers?
- What kind of fear had gripped the house?
- And what were the spiritual forces doing while all this was happening?

This is a spiritual autopsy.

Not a condemnation. A dissection into the facts.

Because when fear enters a house, what we reach for can reveal what—or Who—we truly trust.

And trust, in moments of spiritual crisis, determines alignment.

And alignment determines authority.

Which brings us to one of the questions proposed in this chapter:

Was something shifting in Charlie Kirk's spiritual life?

Let's look at the facts—not speculation but confirmed statements from people close to him.

Candace Owens, a public commentator and former friend of Charlie's, made headlines after his death when she said on her show that Charlie had *"started praying the rosary."*

Why does this matter?

Because that comment didn't just circulate quietly—it became a flashpoint. It went viral, and suddenly people were arguing back and forth online like a spiritual tug-of-war was playing out in real time. And normally, I wouldn't pay attention to that kind of noise. But this time was different.

Candace didn't just mention the rosary. She also said—jokingly— that she once told Charlie he was "too smart to be a Protestant." Many believers, especially Protestants, felt stung by that. And I'll be honest: I would've brushed it off and moved on if it didn't point to something bigger.

But it did.

Because the truth is, when someone puts their trust in Jesus Christ, we're family. And families sometimes have uncomfortable, honest conversations—not to divide, but to understand. And watching the reaction online, I realized this wasn't just about a rosary. There was a deeper issue underneath the surface, and it needed to be addressed, especially in a spiritual autopsy.

And here's what made me pause: Charlie had spent years debating Catholics and explaining why he held Protestant convictions. He was very clear about where he stood. But in those final months, something seemed to have shifted, whether in language, relationships, practices, or simply in the influences around him.

These details might matter—or they may be insignificant. But a real investigation demands we review the evidence honestly.

So I dug deeper. Not to criticize. Not to stir division. But because if we're going to examine what shaped the final weeks of Charlie's spiritual life, we can't skip over something this significant.

According to a Sept. 19, 2025, article in *Catholic News Agency*, Charlie Kirk had what was described as a "personal exchange" with Bishop Joseph Brennan of Fresno, California, just days before his assassination.

The meeting reportedly took place at a prayer breakfast in Visalia, where Charlie shared with the bishop that he had a Catholic wife and children, and that he had been attending Mass with them.

The most striking detail from the article came in Charlie's own words.

The article claimed that Charlie acknowledged the "speculation" surrounding his potential conversion to Catholicism; Charlie reportedly replied: "I'm this close."

That phrase—just two words—is now being interpreted in many different ways.

Was he speaking about conversion? About timing? About death?

We don't know the context.

But the timing is haunting.

Some see it as a moment of clarity.

Others as a moment of curiosity.

Still others have seized on it as a definitive declaration that Charlie Kirk was on the verge of converting.

What's clear is that Catholic commentators wasted no time stepping into the narrative.

Mere hours after his death, Catholic publications and influencers were already positioning Charlie's journey as "proof" of his embrace of Catholic doctrine—including Marian veneration, something he had indeed discussed critically and thoughtfully in one of his final videos.

But whether he was simply exploring…or truly about to convert… we may never know.

Whether Charlie was exploring faith more deeply or simply loving his wife by worshipping with her, we don't know. That isn't the issue here. The issue is what fear does when faith feels uncertain.

What we do know is that many Catholic commentators celebrated | 141 the possibility—and they did so quickly.

And that timing matters.

Now, it's important to note here that Candace Owens has said a lot of controversial things. So take her words with the appropriate grain of salt.

But even so…she wasn't the only one saying it.

When Candace and others began mentioning Charlie and the rosary, it wasn't so much the topic itself that struck me—it was the timing.

Literally within minutes of his death, people were already stepping forward to define what Charlie did or didn't believe, to frame his faith journey for him.

I found that bizarre.

Not because it was Catholic.

Not because it was Protestant.

But because it was immediate.

In the middle of grief and shock, narratives were being shaped about Charlie's soul before his body was even at rest.

Others began posting photos of Charlie and Erika attending Catholic Mass at St. Bernadette's in Scottsdale. There were reports of them visiting the National Basilica in D.C. around that same timeframe.

And then the big one dropped:

It has been reported that Charlie and Erika's marriage was convalidated in the Catholic Church—some asserting this happened in September 2025, the month he was murdered.

But publicly available documentation is lacking.

That said, after years of being married without a Catholic blessing, the timing raises a question: coincidence? Or a pattern pointing to a deeper shift? You decide.

For those who don't know, "convalidation" is a process where the Catholic Church blesses a marriage that previously wasn't considered sacramentally valid in their eyes. It's a way of retroactively bringing a couple into full sacramental alignment—so they can receive the Eucharist.

And then came something even more telling.

John Yep, the president of Catholics for Catholics, shared publicly that he had exchanged direct text messages with Charlie.

In one, Charlie reportedly said, "We need all the Catholics praying the rosary for Trump in 2024."

John responded with Marian images—pictures of the Virgin Mary, commonly used in Catholic devotionals.

According to John, these conversations weren't isolated; they reflected an ongoing spiritual dialogue.

In other words…something was shifting.

Now, out of professional responsibility, it's important to note that Charlie Kirk was a unifier.

He was attempting something that not many before him had tried—to build a political and spiritual bridge between Protestants and Catholics in hopes of rallying unified support for President Donald Trump in key battleground states ahead of the 2024 election.

His effort wasn't about tearing down walls of doctrine. It was, in part, about strategy.

Unity.

Influence.

Victory.

But spiritually speaking…were certain lines getting blurred?

Let's go deeper.

Because now we're stepping into the part of this autopsy I call the Indictment.

But let me be clear before we go any further: this part isn't about Charlie, or his family, or anyone who loved him. This has nothing to do with assigning blame to a person. This section is about something much bigger—about religion, confusion, spiritual drift, and the complicated state of the modern Church.

You've glimpsed the scene.

You've heard the facts.

You've felt the weight.

But now we must ask: who—or what—is to blame?

To answer that question, I need to take you into the future. To the book of Revelation. This moment hasn't happened yet.

But it will.

It's the final showdown between Christ and all evil.

The scene reads like the script of an apocalyptic movie—

angels, judgments, dragons, trumpets—

but it's not just fire and fury.

It's courtroom language.

And this time, Jesus isn't coming as a suffering Savior.

He's coming as a Judge.

See, the first time He came—over 2,000 years ago—He arrived as a lamb.

Full of grace.

Forgiving.

Compassionate.

But the second time?
He's coming to clean house.

And here's what's shocking:
His biggest indictment isn't toward atheists.
Not toward the media.
Not even toward corrupt politicians.

It's toward…the Church.

Not the faithful Church.
Not the pure Church.
Not the Bride that stayed close.
But the lukewarm Church.

Let me show you what He said:
"I know your deeds, that you are neither cold nor hot. I wish you were either one or the other! So, because you are lukewarm—neither hot nor cold—I am about to spit you out of my mouth." —Revelation 3:15–16 NIV

Now pause.
Let that hit.
Jesus literally says: *lukewarm makes Him nauseous.*
Think about that.

If you hand God hot water, He can make something out of it—maybe a strong, healing tea.

If you hand Him ice water, He can work with that too—maybe a cold, refreshing lemonade.

But lukewarm?

He spits it out.

That's not apathy.
That's a divine gag reflex.

Lukewarm isn't ignorance.
It's indecision.
It's someone trying to live in both camps—just enough Jesus to soothe your guilt, just enough compromise to keep your options open.
And the result?
No fire.
No power.

Now keep that in mind, because in Revelation 2:20 NIV, Jesus gives an even sharper rebuke:

"Nevertheless, I have this against you: You tolerate that woman Jezebel, who calls herself a prophet. By her teaching she misleads my servants into sexual immorality and the eating of food sacrificed to idols."
The Bible doesn't just warn about Jezebel and Balaam—
it warns that the Church would
TOLERATE THEM.

Exhibit A: Jezebel.

Yes—the very same name as the magazine that bragged about cursing Charlie Kirk.
The same name.
The same spirit.
The same manipulation.
But this time, He's not talking about an Old Testament queen or a magazine.
He's talking about a Church.
A Church that allowed Jezebel's seduction to twist their theology.

A Church that let her spirit influence their decisions.

A Church that welcomed mixture.

Let me ask you something.
Do you think it's a coincidence that a magazine called *Jezebel* published a hit piece in 2025 celebrating paid curses being placed on Charlie Kirk…just days before his assassination?

Do you think it's a coincidence that the Jezebel of old once sent death threats to Elijah—the boldest prophet of his generation—causing him to run into hiding?

Do you think it's a coincidence that in the final forty-eight hours of Charlie's life, after reading *Jezebel's* curses, fear entered his home?

You can't make this stuff up.

This is not fiction.

This is a pattern.

And the Bible predicted it.

But Jezebel isn't acting alone.

Enter Exhibit B: Balaam, Jezebel's Co-Conspirator.

Now, Balaam is one of the strangest figures in the Bible.

He's a prophet for hire.

Hired by a pagan king to curse the Israelites.

But every time he opens his mouth, he blesses them instead.

He says, "How can I curse what God has blessed?"

(Numbers 23:8 NKJV)

But Balaam didn't give up.

He just changed strategies.

If you can't curse from the outside…infect from the inside.

So Balaam gives the king a plan:

Send in seductive women.

Tempt the men.

Entice them to join pagan rituals.

Get them to mix worship—blend purity with poison.

It worked.

And Israel, once blessed beyond measure, invited their own curse through spiritual compromise.

Here's the shocking part: Jesus mentions both Jezebel and Balaam in Revelation.

"There are some among you who hold to the teaching of Balaam, who taught Balak to entice the Israelites to sin…"

— Revelation 2:14 NIV

Do you see the connection?

• Jezebel used threats, seduction, and fear.

- Balaam used strategy, money, and compromise.

One deceived through domination.

The other deceived through tolerance.

And both, Jesus says, were tolerated by parts of the Church.

So what does this mean for us?

Well—if Jezebel represents a spirit of manipulation and intimidation, and Balaam represents strategic deception through compromise…

…then syncretism is the result.

Syncretism is when you try to mix two things that were never meant to blend.

Light and darkness.

Truth and error.

Yahweh and Baal.

Jesus and fear.

The Holy Spirit and man-made tradition.

The Gospel…and a different gospel.

It's spiritual adultery.

It's mixing altars.

It's saying you trust God—while secretly saving a seat for Plan B.

Idolatry is cheating on God. And God doesn't tolerate that because He's insecure. He refuses to tolerate it because it puts you in danger. Let me explain.

Which brings us to the word that God hates: idolatry.

And no, I don't mean the hit TV show—American Idol.

I'm talking about the eight-letter word that makes the heavens tremble.

Idolatry.

Because idolatry isn't just bowing to statues or burning incense in foreign temples.

It's trusting something else to protect you.

It's running to something else when fear shows up.

It's putting anything—or anyone—in the place only God should hold.

Imagine a wife.
She's loyal.
Committed.
But one day, she starts flirting with a guy at the grocery store.
It starts off innocent.
Small talk.
Compliments.

But the guy is seductive.
Smooth.
Charming.

She starts meeting him every Tuesday in aisle 4.
Eventually…she ends up in his bed.
She still comes home to her husband.
Still sleeps in her marital bed.

But she's now in two beds.

One of them, sacred.
The other? Deadly.

What she doesn't know is the stranger is a murderer.
He's diseased.
Violent.
Evil.
He infects her with something she didn't ask for—something that slowly begins to destroy her from the inside out.
We'd call that an STD—
but let's call it what it is:
a **Spiritually Transmitted Disease**.

Because when you lay with idols…you inherit their consequences.
Now when her life falls apart, she cries out to her husband.
But she's no longer under his roof.
No longer under his protection.
And even though he still loves her…he can't stop the storm she invited.
That's what idolatry does.

It moves you out from God's covering.
It exposes you to danger.

It lets in spirits you weren't meant to host.
God calls Himself "jealous" not because He's controlling—
but because He's protective.

Oprah once described in an interview how, at age twenty-seven or twenty-eight, she was sitting in church listening to a charismatic minister preach about God's greatness and omnipresence.

Everything moved her—until he said, "The Lord thy God is a jealous God."

At that moment, she recalled, something didn't feel right in her spirit.

"God is jealous of me?" she thought.

That phrase, she said, didn't sit right with her.

Unfortunately, she misunderstood the word.

Because God's jealousy isn't petty.

It's passionate.

In the original language it means: an ardent, protective zeal—an intense commitment of a covenant partner who refuses rival claims on the beloved.

It's the kind of jealousy that says:

"You were made to be Mine, and I won't stand by while you destroy yourself."

In a culture where some men take pleasure in watching their wives sleep with other men—and call it freedom—

is it any wonder why the idea of a jealous God feels offensive?

Because if your definition of love has been shaped by porn, betrayal, or platform performance...

then of course covenant will feel like control.

Of course holiness will feel heavy.

Of course jealousy will feel...toxic.

| 149

But that's not the jealousy of God.

His jealousy doesn't wound.
It shields.

It doesn't imprison.
It protects.

God doesn't want your performance.
He wants to be your protection.

And He can't protect what isn't aligned with Him.

Let's talk about the word *apostasy*.

You've probably heard it thrown around in sermons or Christian podcasts, but let me break it down in plain terms.

Apostasy is not struggling with your faith.

Apostasy isn't failure.

It's betrayal.

It's not wrestling with God in the middle of the night.

It's not even falling into sin out of weakness.

It's far more dangerous.

Apostasy is when someone knows what the Bible says…

…has built systems on it, preached it, enforced it for generations…

…and then publicly rejects it—in favor of cultural accommodation or personal preference.

It's not confusion.

It's spiritual corruption.

Now take a moment and let's examine that through the lens of the spiritual autopsy we're performing.

And I ask this respectfully, for investigative purposes only:

What if Charlie's final days were clouded not just by political stress or personal exhaustion…

but by a spiritual fog?

What if fear crept in through an open window—

one the Church should have shut?

And what if that fear wasn't just emotional…

but demonic torment?

I'm not saying the man was possessed.

I'm saying our thoughts can sometimes be influenced by dark forces if we're not careful.

Only God knows…

That brings us back to Revelation.

When Jesus calls out the Church of Thyatira, He isn't just venting.

He's giving us a blueprint for what goes wrong when tolerance replaces truth.

Thyatira, by the way, literally means "the choice of the people."
Let me say that again.
The church Jesus rebukes for tolerating Jezebel was literally named the people's choice.
Not God's choice.

The people's choice.

That's what happens when church becomes a popularity contest.
When sermons are shaped by applause instead of anointing.

When theology is based on trends instead of truth.

When leaders look to polls, not the presence of God.

It becomes a religion of the crowd.

A church of compromise.

And that's what Jesus was indicting in Revelation.

He said, "You've tolerated Jezebel.
You've tolerated Balaam.
You've allowed spiritual adultery in My house.
You've opened the door to mixture.
And now, you're lukewarm."

And here's the sobering reality:
When the Church tolerates what God never approved,
the devil doesn't have to break in.
He's been invited.

So who's to blame?
Who should bear the weight of Charlie Kirk's assassination?
Was it the shooter?
The witches?
The Church?

Honestly...that's a hard question.
But maybe the better question is: *who wasn't activated?*

Let me revisit the quote that's been floating around in the circles of conservative Christians for years:
"If the pastors had done their jobs, Charlie Kirk wouldn't have one."

That's not a knock on Charlie.

It's a compliment.

It means he was stepping into territory that the pulpits had abandoned.

He was standing in cultural gaps where the Church had fallen silent.

He was confronting deception where many pastors had chosen comfort.

But maybe that was never supposed to be his job in the first place.

Charlie himself once questioned the Church's inactivity.

In a *Turning Point USA Faith* video titled "Is the Church Getting Lazy," he and Pastor Tommy Barnett had a conversation about how many believers had spiritually fallen asleep.

The question wasn't just rhetorical.

It was prophetic.

And tragically, that same question has now become part of this autopsy.

Because while witches were conjuring, some Christians were compromising.

While spiritual assignments were being spoken, some pulpits were silent.

While Erika was shaken, some in the Church were sleeping.

And that should grieve us.

Not because we need to condemn anyone—especially not those closest to Charlie—

but because we must wake up to the war we're in.

A war where deception is dressed in spirituality.

Where the voice of God is muffled by mixture.

So now we come to the final verdict.

Not on Charlie.

Not on his team.

Not on the priest.

Not on Protestants.

Not on Catholics.

But on the spiritual system that allowed Jezebel and Balaam to re-enter the story...and go unchallenged.

This is about gaps.
And who didn't fill them.

Because Revelation tells us exactly where this ends.
The lukewarm Church—

not the atheist,

not the witch,

not the activist—

the lukewarm Church
gets spit out.

And that's not God being cruel.
That's God being holy.

Because mixture pollutes power.
And lukewarm faith leads people to hell just as much as outright rebellion.

So I challenge you…
Not to pick a side in the Protestant-Catholic debate.
Not to blame a person, a podcast, or a priest.
But to ask yourself:
- Where have I tolerated this spirit of Jezebel?
- Where have I let Balaam whisper strategy into my thinking?
- Where have I opened my door to fear and called it wisdom?
- Where have I mixed truth with compromise?
- Where have I become…lukewarm?

Because if Charlie's murder doesn't wake us up, then what will?
This isn't about blaming each other.
Because our fight isn't with flesh and blood—it's a spiritual one. | 153
We don't know what people prayed.
We don't know what they saw.
We don't know what they carried, what they whispered, or how they fought behind the scenes.
The Bible says, "Man looks at the outward appearance, but the LORD looks at the heart" (1 Samuel 16:7 NKJV).
And that's where judgment belongs—with God alone.
So this isn't about condemnation.
It's about confrontation.

Not of people…but of the spirits behind the pattern.

Because if you really trace it back—

if you really follow the trail of breadcrumbs from *Jezebel*'s article to the priest's prayer to the echoing silence in the Church—

you won't find a list of guilty names.

You'll find a pattern that runs through the centuries—one that connects kings and prophets, presidents and pop stars, pastors and pew-sitters, famous people and everyday people like you and me.

A little mixture.

A little confusion.

A little fear.

And before long, you're in bed with something that doesn't love you back.

Could this be why so many of us can agree that our current culture feels over-sexualized?

Look at the commercials on TV—the constant parade of half-naked bodies.

Look at the culture of the selfie—influencers rewarded for posting what used to be private.

Corporate endorsements and viral fame now flow to whoever shows the most skin.

Married men and married women are forced to be careful how they scroll—a single flick of the thumb now opens portals to temptation.

Dating apps have made adultery easier, faster, and more anonymous than at any point in history.

Is this random? Or is there something—or Someone—more sinister at play here?

Has Jezebel's spirit expanded from ancient kings to algorithms?

A seduction so slow you don't even notice it happening.

A Jezebel spirit not just whispering to kings but to all of us, nudging us toward compromise.

Not just another person's bed, but another altar.

What used to be shameful…is now sponsored.

Do you see what's happening?
They've flipped the script.

What used to be spiritually dangerous…is now marketed as self-care.
What once required repentance…is now rebranded as empowerment.

That's why we already told the parable.
You remember—the wife who flirted in aisle four. Who slept in two beds. Who thought she could manage compromise without consequence.
It didn't start violent.
It didn't start obvious.
It started with a compliment.

And that's the pattern of idolatry.

That's how demons dress themselves in religious clothes.
That's how seducing spirits sound like affirmation.
That's how compromise gets labeled "wisdom."

And slowly…even the Bride of Christ forgets who she belongs to.
That's where we are.

This is the autopsy report.

A fear-soaked culture.
A truth-starved Church.
A celebrity-driven Christianity that has blurred the line between influence and intimacy.

And if you want the real indictment…here it is:

It's not on Charlie.
It's not his friends.
It's not some conspiracy theory spread by Candace Owens.
It's not on the witches or the warlocks or even the wicked.

When it's all said and done…
The real indictment is on the systems we've tolerated.
The idols we've flirted with.

It's on the part of the body that can quote politics but not Scripture.

It's on the rituals that put space between us and God.

It's on the silent pulpits, yes—but also the silent pews.

It's on a generation that knows how to produce podcasts but not how to prophesy in power.

Because while Jezebel was hurling threats...
          ...we were arguing over coffee flavors in the church lobby.
While curses were being spoken...
    ...we were scrolling.
While Charlie's family was rattled...
    ...many of us were distracted.
While darkness organized...
    ...too many believers were divided.

And no, we're not saying it's your fault.
Or mine.
Or any single person's.

But what if it's been all of us?
What if this isn't a moment to point fingers—
but for deep reflection?
Because let's be real:

If a magazine named *Jezebel* is publishing articles bragging about paid witches cursing Christians...

...and the Church doesn't flinch...

...then what have we become?

If fear can enter a home and no one stands in authority...

...then what are we really preaching?

If the Bride—the Church—can flirt and no one notices she's missing...

...then who's really watching the door?

Let me say it as clearly as I can:

This chapter isn't about pointing outward.

It's about examining inward.

It's about pulling the curtain back on a system that has normalized lukewarm.

And the book of Revelation already told us what happens next.

The lukewarm get spit out.

Not because God is cruel.

Because God is holy.

Mixture pollutes authority.

Compromise weakens the covering.

And fear…opens the door.

Fear opened doors for JFK, Michael Jackson, John Lennon, Job, and many others.

We've seen what fear can do in the lives of people.

But here's the antithesis of fear—perfect love.

Even I once slept with weapons—a machete under my pillow.

Living in fear.

Mixed with the wrong people.

Reaping consequences I thought I couldn't escape.

Until I read the Scripture that changed everything:

"There is no fear in love. But perfect love casts out fear, because fear has to do with punishment. The one who fears is not made perfect in love."
—1 John 4:18 NIV

And that's the silver lining here. | 157

Because after all the theology, the debates, the doctrines—none of that will matter.

When it's all said and done, even in Revelation's final showdown—when Good finally defeats evil—

God doesn't end the story with thunder.

It fades to candlelight on a dinner table.

The camera pans from the chaos of headlines to the quiet of a single door.

But even here—in the hush between judgment and mercy—comes a knock.

Not a slam.

Not a shout.

Not a fireball from heaven.

Just…a knock.

"Behold, I stand at the door and knock. If anyone hears My voice and opens the door, I will come in and dine with him, and he with Me."
—Revelation 3:20 NKJV

So let's pause for a moment.
Really let this sink in.
This isn't just an interesting theory or a theological footnote.
It's a spiritual bombshell.

While Jezebel is hurling threats…

while witchcraft and sexuality are being *weaponized*…

while Balaam's strategy is still *seducing* the Church into idolatry and apostasy…

The God who spoke the universe into existence is at your door—
not to destroy you,
but to have dinner with you.

So what—or who—in the world could stop you from opening that door?

Fear?

Shame?

Religion?

None of them can stand between you and the knock.
As we look back at the evidence board—at the tree in the garden of Eden—we remember:
He wasn't surprised when the first humans failed.
He already had a rescue plan.

So if He wasn't shocked in Eden,
He's not shocked by your own story either.

That means nothing you've done disqualifies you from answering.
Not your record.

Not your theology.

Not your denomination.

Think about that.
After all the mixture.
After all the compromise.
After all the cheating…
Jesus is still knocking.
He still wants dinner.

He still wants you.

No rituals.

  No credentials.

    Just hunger.

      Because in the end, it's not the witches who win.

        It's not the spirits who write the final page.

          It's not the seduction that gets the last say.

It's the One at the door.

And He's not knocking to condemn you.
He's knocking to feed you.
To welcome you back.

But here's the catch.
You can't stay in both beds.
You can't sleep with idols on Tuesday and eat with the King on Sunday.
You can't straddle two altars and call it faith.

So let me end this first part of the spiritual investigation the only way I can.

Let me ask you one last time:

Are you hungry?

Because if you are…
The table is set.
He's knocking at the door.

And the only way to the feast…

Is to leave the other bed…

…and to just—come home.

9

GOD KNEW...BUT DID HE WANT IT?

The Devil's Alibi

"Even if His fingerprints are at the crime scene, it doesn't mean He pulled the trigger." — Stevie Prince

This investigation leads us back to the White House—during one of the most pivotal crossroads in American history.

And regardless of whether you failed history class or slept through it, what happened in this scene matters more than most people realize.

It's early morning in Washington, 1862.

A horse-drawn carriage stops at the gates of the most powerful house in the country.

The air is cold, the city still waking from a night heavy with war telegrams and exhaustion.

Soldiers stand in silence as a small coffin is lifted and carried inside.

Not the coffin of a president or a general,

but of a child—

eleven-year-old *William Wallace Lincoln*,

the second son of Abraham and Mary Todd Lincoln.

Inside the East Room, mirrors are covered in black cloth.

The smell of lilies fills the air.

I imagine the President standing motionless while his wife trembles beneath a veil.

Imagine her in that moment—hearing the creak of the pew, the whisper of her own heartbeat, and realizing that the same God she once thanked for victory is now being preached as the One who permitted her loss.

Reverend Phineas D. Gurley, the Lincolns' pastor, opens his notes and begins to speak:

Disease and death are His messengers; they go forth at His bidding, and their fearful work is limited or extended, according to the good pleasure of His will.

The nation needed theology that explained everything.
But for a grieving mother, those words hit like nails.
That morning, theology did what bullets could not—it framed God; it made Him look guilty.
I can imagine her staring ahead, hearing every syllable and wondering what kind of Father calls this good.
That morning, theology tried to comfort the crowd—

and instead made God look complicit.

Maybe you've been in a room like that.
Not a state funeral, but your own private room.
A moment when someone wrapped your pain in a verse and called it God's plan.
You nodded politely while your heart screamed,
Then why didn't He stop it?

We've all been there—when the One who's supposed to protect us seems to sign the permission slip for our heartbreak.
So the question becomes:
What would lead the First Lady of the United States to later sit with mediums, searching for voices on the other side?

As we revisited this moment and pulled excerpts from Gurley's sermon, new clues started to surface—details most historians mention only in passing.
Together they paint a picture of one of the most unjust moments in spiritual history:

the day God Himself was put on trial in the court of human pain.
To frame someone means to make an innocent person appear guilty—

to stage the evidence, twist the story,
and hang the verdict on the wrong name.

Movies didn't invent that storyline; they just copied it.

Think of *The Dark Knight*, when Batman takes the blame for another man's crimes so the city can keep its hope intact.

Think of *The Fugitive*, or *The Shawshank Redemption*, or *Minority Report*—each built on the agony of being accused of something you didn't do.

We watch because every one of us knows that feeling.

Have you ever been blamed for something you didn't do?

Maybe a sibling left the toilet seat up and you took the fall.

Maybe your coworker dropped the ball and your name hit the report.

Maybe someone swore you said something you never said.

It sounds trivial until you've lived it—

that twist in your stomach when the truth doesn't matter because the story's already been written.

Now imagine that on a cosmic scale.

The real villain commits the act
and pins it on heaven.
Evil gets an alibi.
God gets the blame.

Maybe the reason that moment haunts me is because I've stood in that same room—different century, same silence.

When the one you trusted to protect you stands frozen, and the theology you grew up with sounds like an alibi instead of comfort.

My Exhibit A

I know something about that frame.

I was sixteen when I started to believe the architect of my pain might be my own father.

He was a good man—respected, busy, my hero.

I was seventeen the day that question moved from theory to blood.

My father was a pastor—a strong voice behind pulpits, the man everyone called for advice.

My hero. Until he became president of our church organization and the ground shifted under our family. His new role meant leaving the church that had raised me—the friends I'd grown up with, the piano bench where I first felt purpose.

I begged to stay.

He said, "This is my ministry. You'll follow me."

But I couldn't.

A new pastor took over our church.

To me, he was an intruder wearing my father's suit.

One week I skipped church on a Sunday—I left town to play piano at a wedding; the next, I was summoned before him and a room of deacons.

"If you don't call me Pastor, you'll never play here again."

I went home furious and told my dad.

He was lying in bed, exhausted from flights and meetings.

"I'll talk to him," he said.

He never did.

And just like that, the man I thought would fight for me went silent.

Soon the calls involving me with church events stopped.

The invitations vanished.

The same people who'd once cheered for me now whispered— mean rumors about me.

I felt like an outcast who had contracted leprosy.

And my father?

Having coffee with the very men who'd humiliated me.

Maybe you know that ache—
the slow betrayal that doesn't explode but erodes.

When someone who could have defended you…doesn't.

You start to wonder if they let it happen.

If they planned it.

If the architect of your safety drew the blueprints for your fall.

That's when intimacy dies.

You can't sing beside someone you no longer trust to protect you.

You can't call home the place where the wound was signed.

So I stopped going.

For years I refused to step inside a church. The stage that once felt like purpose now felt like a crime scene. I buried my piano keys and picked up new addictions instead—

beds, bodies, blurred nights—

anything that let me control the ending for once.

I called it freedom; it was grief in disguise.

My dad wasn't God.
He made mistakes—human ones that still echo.
But pain with an earthly father has a way of rewriting how we see the heavenly One.
If the man who raised me could stay silent, maybe God would too.

If my father's inaction could cost me my song, maybe God's could cost me more.

That's how the framing happens.
The enemy doesn't need to destroy your faith; he only needs to distort your view of the Father.
He whispers through pulpits and funerals and childhood wounds:

"See? He planned it. He wanted it."

And before long, you stop running *to* Him—
and start running *from* Him.

I began to wonder if that's what Mary Todd Lincoln felt in that East Room.
That shock and betrayal…What I felt at sixteen.
Maybe that's what you've felt before too.

Let's frame this picture from a different perspective…
Imagine a crime scene.

A body. A weapon. Two sets of fingerprints.
If you're the investigator, the conclusion seems obvious: two people were involved—one pulled the trigger, the other helped.
But the evidence tells a stranger story.

Only one killer.

The second set of prints belonged to someone who was there—watching, present, but restrained.

A witness bound by His own word.

That seems to be the paradox of humanity.

From the beginning, the evidence has pointed to a Creator-Judge who was both witness and lawgiver.

Not absent. Not powerless. But limited—by His own integrity.

When He gave humanity free will, He embedded mystery into the system itself.

The fingerprints of both mercy and malice trace back to that single gift: free will.

And as you'll uncover in Chapter 13, the human will seems to be at the center of a cosmic trial between good and evil—while humanity stands in the crosshairs.

It's the oldest case in creation.

And the evidence keeps circling back to the same question:

If God knew what would happen, did He want it to happen?

Now pause for a second.

Imagine yourself as God.

Not in a blasphemous way—just for perspective.

Imagine that every word you speak becomes law.

Remember the movie *Bruce Almighty*? Jim Carrey plays a man who thinks he can run the universe better than God.

So God—played by Morgan Freeman—hands him the keys, temporarily.

What follows is chaos.

Because every wish, every complaint, every careless word Jim Carrey's character speaks becomes reality.

It's played for comedy, but the implications are profound.

Imagine you step outside one morning, look up at the sky, and jokingly declare, "Let chocolate M&Ms fall from heaven."

And suddenly they do.

Now imagine that moment multiplied by infinity—by the power of a perfect, eternal being whose words form galaxies.

Even the world's economists admit that when a president of the United States tweets a single sentence, global markets react.

Stocks rise or collapse on one phrase.

If the words of a man can move markets—what could the words of God move?

Planets?

Atoms?

Time itself?

That's the dilemma of omnipotence.

A God whose voice creates worlds cannot speak carelessly. Every word He utters sets reality in motion.

So what does He do?

He delegates.

As we've explored in earlier chapters, Genesis records the moment when God said,

"Let Us make man in Our image."
—Genesis 1:26 NKJV

And with those words, He transferred a measure of His creative power—dominion, authority, choice.

Think about it...

That moment wasn't symbolic—it was legal.

A divine handoff.

Humanity became a co-signer on creation's contract.

And since that day, no other species has shared the same ability: to reason, to speak, to imagine, to decree.

Science calls it consciousness.

Scripture calls it image-bearing.

So if humans truly bear God's image—if our words and choices echo His creative power—then here's a question most theologians are afraid to ask:

Could God's decision to give humans dominion have also created divine restraint?

Could the Creator's own integrity limit what He can or cannot do—without violating His own design?

Yeah.
That should make us stop.
Because if that's true—if divine restraint is real—then the question that haunts every tragedy suddenly feels even heavier.
We've all asked it.

When the unthinkable happens.

When evil seems to win.

When good men die and God stays silent.

Where was He?

Every generation reopens the same case file, hoping to find something new in the evidence. Some blame God for pulling the trigger. Others insist He wasn't even there.
But what if the truth is far more complicated—

that He was present all along, bound by His own gift, watching humanity wield the very freedom He gave us?

We've all asked it.
Some whisper it through tears, others shout it into the night.
Those same three little words that echo across hospital rooms and headlines alike:

Where was God?

Where was God when the company downsized and the bills kept coming?
Where was God when my marriage cracked, when my best friend betrayed me, when the doctor said "terminal"?
In other words, maybe your empty line is different—
Where was God when _____ happened?

You don't have to be religious to feel that ache.

Things get even more troubling if the question transitions from "Where was God?" to "Was this tragedy God's will?"

It goes from Maybe God was on vacation or caught by surprise, to God was complicit.

That cuts even deeper.

I began to see that maybe evil itself twisted truth—realizing that God was restrained by His own gift of freedom to humanity, and with the help of religion, framed the wrong picture.

So is there something deeper going on here?

And now, a nation asks:

Where was God when a man named Charlie Kirk was murdered in broad daylight—his wife watching, his audience stunned, millions seeing it unfold live?

As I've mentioned in other chapters, this story is about far more than one man.

Whether you were a fan or a critic, we've all been there—we've all faced that same question: why was something painful allowed to happen to us?

And since every news outlet has already tried to spin its own version of the Charlie Kirk tragedy, this book won't add to the noise.

We'll dig deeper—continue to follow the evidence. The patterns and spiritual threads may shock you by the time you reach the end of this book. Because at the core of it all, beyond headlines and politics, one truth remains:

A father gunned down on stage is evil.
Period.

And I'll take it even further—

unnecessary wars, Christians murdered in Nigeria,

children indoctrinated by demons,

the innocent traded for profit—it's all evil.

Different stage, same spirit.

And sometimes that spirit doesn't hide in back alleys or ancient wars—it walks onto platforms, into pulpits, and behind podiums.

It showed up again in Butler, Pennsylvania.

And yet, in the months that followed, another viral question rose from every pulpit and podcast:

Why did God save Donald Trump in Butler, Pennsylvania…but not Charlie Kirk?

Some asked it gently, through tears.
Internet prophets delivered their verdicts like prosecutors:
"God spared Trump because his mission wasn't finished—but He took Charlie because his was."

Those words landed like shrapnel.
If that's true, then heaven runs on a lottery system—where one man gets angels and another gets bullets.

Is that who God is?
Or are we missing something?

That's the question that haunts me.
And maybe it should haunt the Church too.

During this spiritual investigation, I started hearing YouTube prophets explaining that God was "All Sovereign" and that He left us "prophetic clues."

Something about that narrative didn't feel right—the comparison between President Trump and Charlie Kirk.

Before we dig in, a little context about that day—July 13, 2024, in Butler, Pennsylvania. President Donald Trump was speaking to a crowd when a shooter opened fire.

Secret Service agents tackled the president.

A bullet grazed his ear.

He lived.

Then, more than a year later, Charlie Kirk was assassinated in another city—one whose name, translated, carries imagery of the dragon or the crafty snake (explained in prior chapters).

Some claim the symbolism practically screams of spiritual warfare.

So maybe God did leave clues.

Maybe both events carried prophetic fingerprints.

Just because God's fingerprints are at the crime scene doesn't mean He pulled the trigger.

To break this down: many people believe if God is God, He knows all things before they happen—which is true.
But here's the tension:

Foreknowledge is not authorship.

Prophecy reveals potential, not permission.

The clues God leaves are often warnings, not endorsements.

To understand why this tension keeps resurfacing, we have to step back—way back—before Butler or Babylon—and trace humanity's oldest question: Who is running this story?
Since the first sunrise, mankind has been searching for meaning.
In ancient Babylon, the earliest known writing—cuneiform—told of gods of sun and storm. In Egypt, hieroglyphs covered tombs with prayers to Ra and Osiris. In Greece, poets wrote of Zeus hurling lightning bolts and Hercules wrestling monsters.
Every culture built its own bridge to heaven.
Why?
Because something deep inside us insists there's more.
The ache for meaning isn't a flaw of evolution; it's the fingerprint of eternity.
Every temple raised, every idol carved, every song sung to the sky—it's all an echo of what Ecclesiastes 3:11 NIV declared long ago:
"He has made everything beautiful in its time.
He has also set eternity in the human heart,
yet no one can fathom what God has done from beginning to end."

Even skeptics feel it—that pull toward purpose.

Centuries later, Paul, once a persecutor of Christians turned apostle, wrote to the Romans:
"Since the creation of the world God's invisible qualities—his eternal power and divine nature—have been clearly seen, being understood from what has been made" (Romans 1:20 NIV).

Translation: creation itself testifies.

Mountains, galaxies, the rhythm of your own heartbeat—they all whisper, Someone made this.

Then Paul stood on Mars Hill in Athens, the Silicon Valley of philosophy, surrounded by idols.

He pointed to an altar inscribed TO AN UNKNOWN GOD and said:

> "From one man he made all nations…he marked out their appointed times in history and the boundaries of their lands. God did this so they would seek him and perhaps reach out for him and find him—though he is not far from any one of us." —Acts 17:26–27 NIV

At first glance, that sounds like destiny carved in stone.
But look closer.
The Greek word *kairoi*—"appointed times"—means seasons, not seconds.
Paul wasn't mapping our deaths; he was describing historical windows when nations rise and fall so that people might find God.
In other words:

God orchestrates eras, not executions.
He knows the storm is coming—but that doesn't mean He sends the lightning.

So when we ask, "Did God plan the assassination?" the honest, biblical answer is:

He foresaw it.

He permitted it within the boundaries of human freedom.

But He didn't want it.

Because wanting evil would make Him its author—and that, He can never be.

The Bible is full of this tension.

The people of Israel demanded a king. God warned them it would enslave them. They insisted. So He gave them Saul.

He allowed what He didn't desire.

God knew...but it wasn't His will.

Generations later, a young woman named Esther faced genocide. Her uncle told her, If you remain silent, deliverance will arise from another place—but who knows if you were brought to the kingdom "for such a time as this?"—Esther 4:14 NKJV
She had to decide.
Her silence could have cost a nation.

God knew...but He was waiting for her yes.

Then Jesus.
Standing on a hill overlooking Jerusalem, He wept:
"If you, even you, had only known what on this day would bring you peace—but now it is hidden from your eyes."
—Luke 19:42 NIV

He saw judgment coming.

He prophesied it.

But He didn't want it.

Even the Son of God felt the ache of what could have been.

And Scripture says something even more shocking:
"He did not do many miracles there because of their lack of faith."
—Matthew 13:58 NIV

The all-powerful Christ—limited not by ability but by human agreement.

Heaven's will still needed earth's participation.
That's the prophetic tension—
the collision point between what God knows and what people choose,

between heaven's blueprint and earth's obedience.

And maybe that's what happened in our time.

Maybe Charlie Kirk's death wasn't "God's timing."

Maybe it was hell's timing—and heaven was waiting for someone to interrupt it.

Maybe the angels assigned to protect him were resisted, like the messenger in Daniel 10:12–13 NIV, who told the prophet,
"From the first day you set your heart to understand…your words were heard…but the prince of the Persian kingdom resisted me twenty-one days."

Think about that. From day one, the prayer was answered—yet an unseen war delayed it.

If evil can resist a divine message, why couldn't it resist a divine protection?

Maybe the tragedy wasn't heaven's design, but humanity's silence.

We keep saying, "God, why didn't You intervene?"

Maybe heaven is asking, "Church, why didn't you?"

That's why this moment matters.
It exposes two worldviews still dividing the Church.

One says life runs on a blueprint—every event drawn by the Architect's pen, every tragedy pre-approved in heaven's design.

The other says we're living inside a war zone—where evil can resist, delay, and even corrupt what God intends until someone enforces His will.

Both claim Scripture.
But only one matches the behavior of Jesus.

When Christ walked into chaos, He didn't treat storms, sickness, or demons like coworkers fulfilling a divine schedule.
He rebuked them.

He spoke to fever like an intruder, not an instrument.

He called oppression bondage and set the captive free.

In Luke 4 and again in Luke 13, the Gospels describe Jesus rebuking sickness and demonic torment.
The word used is *epitimáō* (ἐπιτιμάω)—a Greek term meaning "to forbid," "to charge sharply," or "to censure."
It's the same word used when He rebuked the wind and the sea in Mark 4:39.

He didn't comfort the storm; He commanded it.

He didn't negotiate with pain; He issued it a cease-and-desist.

That's why His vocabulary mattered.
Every time He spoke to disease or darkness, His tone was judicial, not sympathetic.
He addressed evil as an unlawful occupant—as if serving an eviction notice to trespassing forces.

Every command.

Every healing.

Every confrontation proved the same truth:

Heaven wasn't conspiring with hell—it was confronting it.

Every confrontation was a reminder:

Heaven was reclaiming occupied territory.

That's why Daniel's vision wasn't mythology; it was a map.
A glimpse of resistance.
Evidence that the blueprint theory explains order, but the warfare reality explains conflict.
And Jesus entered both—
architect of creation,
soldier of redemption.

He proved once and for all that heaven doesn't collaborate with chaos—it conquers it.
And yet, centuries later, we still argue about the verdict.
The war He exposed didn't end on Calvary; it just changed theaters. | 177
Now it plays out in pulpits, podcasts, and politics—
everywhere truth and deception compete for the microphone.
I've spent months watching every clip, every sermon, every so-called prophecy.
Everyone wants to explain it. Some connect dots so fast they create constellations God never drew. Others retreat into clichés—"It was just his time."

But if every bullet and betrayal is pre-scheduled by God, then free will is fiction and love is an illusion.

No—love requires choice.
And choice means risk.

God created beings capable of refusing Him—angels and humans alike. That's not weakness; that's the price of genuine relationship.

He could stop every murderer by erasing freedom—
but He'd also erase love.

So instead, He partners.

He warns.

He waits.

He sends prophets, intercessors, dreamers—people who can sense the danger before it hits and stand in the gap.

But if they sleep through the alarm, evil proceeds unchecked.

Maybe that's what happened.
Maybe the Church hit snooze.

Still, I don't write this to blame.
I write it because I question if heaven was watching that day.
And when the shot rang out, did Jesus weep—just as He did over Jerusalem—

because what could have been…wasn't?

And here's the haunting beauty of it all:

God's foreknowledge doesn't cancel human agency—it magnifies it.

When Jesus walked the earth, He knew Peter would deny Him—and still chose Peter to lead.
He knew Judas would betray Him—and still washed Judas's feet.
He knew every headline, every crime scene, every crucifixion—and still wrote redemption into the script.

That's sovereignty—
not control, but partnership.
Not dictatorship, but invitation.

He lets us co-author history with Him.
And sometimes, tragically, we don't pick up the pen.

So yes, if God is an all-knowing, true God—then God knew.
He wasn't surprised.
He saw the tragedy before it happened.

If we believe what YouTube prophets say—the connection between the locations of the shootings of Donald Trump vs Charlie Kirk—then the conclusion leads us to believe He saw the butler's bullet miss and the dragon's bullet hit.

He saw the prophets speculating, the skeptics mocking, the families grieving.

But what if foreknowledge isn't desire?
And presence at the crime scene isn't participation?

He may have been there—because He's everywhere—
but He wasn't the killer.

He was the Father who'd already handed His children the keys to stop it—watching them destroy each other with the very freedom He gave them.

Tainted evidence was planted.
Evil painted the picture.
Twisted religion framed it.
And heaven took the blame.

Even now, it stops me cold—
As we know—the shirt Charlie wore that day read *FREEDOM.*
The word that once sounded like celebration now feels like a reminder of what heaven refused to violate.

That freedom cost Him everything.
And it still costs us when the Church stays quiet.

Maybe you're still wrestling with that.
Good.
Hold that tension.

So we circle back to the question that's been burning since that funeral in the East Room of the White House—or maybe from your own tragedy:

Who's really running the script?

Now, I brought up the example about my own life and my own father not to throw stones at him—
I've forgiven him—
but to bring an important lesson into the light.

When there's betrayal in a family—
when the ones you love seem to have orchestrated or even colluded with your enemies—
it cracks the very foundation of that family.

And that's what happened with me.
Years later, I carried so much bitterness toward my father.
I could sit at the same Thanksgiving table, smile through holidays, make small talk about weather and work—
but inside there was a gaping hole in my soul.

Questions.

Things that didn't make sense.

The impossibility of any real connection because he still hadn't addressed the things he did to me.

Maybe he didn't realize what he'd done.
Maybe he just didn't care.
I wasn't sure.
What I did know, as a young man trying to build a life, was that it hurt—
and it hurt deep.
I remember reaching one of my lowest moments.
I was visiting my parents when my father said something that triggered me.
Everything went black.
Rage boiled up.
I was sick and tired of the silence, the hypocrisy, the unresolved ache.
I remember grinding my teeth, stepping toward him, grabbing him by his shirt with one hand,
and raising my fist with the other—
as my mother stepped between us, crying, begging me to let him go.

After a few seconds, I released his shirt, stepped back,
and couldn't believe what I'd just done.
The very bitterness toward the father I believed had orchestrated
my pain
had now brought me to this point.
I ran out of that house—angry, confused, broken,
not even understanding what was wrong with me.

It took years before I could finally look back and see what was
really happening.
There was an invisible force behind that moment—
something that had been orchestrating division,
not just in my home but in my heart.
An unseen hand trying to break my family apart.

And maybe you've felt that too—
the pain when your own family wounds you.
Moments that tore your home apart,
times you wish you could replay, rewrite, redo.

So I pivot back to the purpose of this chapter.
Why set God up?
Who would have anything to gain by framing God at the crime
scene?

That's when more dots began to connect.

It wasn't coincidence that soon after the sermon preached by
President Lincoln's pastor—
a sermon that made it sound as though it was God's providence
and will
for such heartbreak to happen inside the White House—
that very same family, sitting in front of their son's coffin,
would turn away from their heavenly Father and look elsewhere
for comfort.
Not my words—his pastor's.

Check the archived sermon for yourself.

Soon thereafter, instead of turning to their Father in heaven,

the President of the United States and the most powerful family
on Earth
turned their hope to mediums—
to a practice God had already forbidden.
Necromancy.
Speaking to the dead.

Depending on your theological background or worldview, some
believe that speaking to the dead is really speaking to demons or
familiar spirits—
entities that disguise themselves as the voices of lost loved ones
in order to deceive and sow confusion.

But that's another story for another day.
The point is this: when false theology—no matter how well-
intentioned—frames God as the author of tragedy, it poisons the
relationship.
Just like it did with me and my father, the bond between son and
father—or daughter and father—turns from trust to resentment.
And once we fall into that trap, we find ourselves doing the same
thing I once did—

attempting to grab God by the shirt,

raising our fist,

grinding our teeth,

not even realizing why we're so angry with Him.

10

THE INHERITANCE CLAUSE

You've Been Served

Power of Attorney: signed in blood

It starts with a knock.

Sharp. Unplanned.

A delivery guy in uniform stands on the porch, envelope in hand. "Signature required."

You're irritated—you were in the middle of something. You sign, barely looking up. He leaves without a word. The sound of the truck fades down the street.

You tear open the envelope like it insulted you.

Inside—letterhead. A law firm you've never heard of.

For a second, your gut drops. Am I in trouble?

You start scanning the page, hunting for whatever you supposedly did wrong. Then you see it—your name.

And three words that change everything:

Last Will and Testament.

He's not a creditor.

Not a collector.

He's family—a name you might've heard once at a reunion or through a rumor. An uncle you never met. And apparently, he left you everything.

Property.

Land.

A beach house.

A vintage car collection.

Accounts, stocks, deeds.

And a mansion that's been in the family for generations.

You flip the envelope over, half expecting to see *Just kidding* printed somewhere in fine print. But it's legit. The seal's embossed. Your name is typed in black ink across the top line.

You didn't earn it.

You didn't ask for it.

But it's yours.

You finally agree to meet with the law firm. You know nothing about estate law—you've only seen it in movies.

Lucky heirs. Billionaires. Long-lost relatives.

That's not your life. At least, not until now.

You're sitting in the waiting room. The attorney steps out, shakes your hand, calls you by your last name. He leads you into a conference room, offers a cup of stale coffee. You politely decline.

You just want the facts.

You sit across from him at a table big enough for board meetings. He slides the paperwork across. You don't understand half of it—it's legal mumbo jumbo.

But one thing is clear: Your uncle did pretty well.

He hands you a pen. "Sign on the dotted line."

That's it.

One signature.

And your life changes forever.

You sit there, holding the paperwork, feeling like reality hasn't caught up yet.

The attorney shakes your hand, slips you his business card, and says, "If you ever need help planning your estate, give me a call."

You nod. You walk out with a manila folder full of documents—

bank accounts, property deeds, addresses, and keys to places you've never been.

You get in your car. Pull up the GPS. Type in the address printed on the first page of the will.

You start driving toward a city you've never been to. The closer you get, the less real it feels.

You pull up to the gate.

Your phone speaks: "Arrived."

This is it.

Your new home.

You double-check the address—three times. Four, if you count the phone call to the attorney.

He chuckles. "You're at the right place. Technically, it's yours now. But you might have to deal with squatters."

Squatters.

The word hits different when it's your property they're in.

What's a squatter?

Squatter (noun): someone occupying property without legal ownership or permission.

You stare at the gates. The lawn's overgrown.

Windows cracked. And through the glass, silhouettes move. People inside.

Your jaw tightens.

The paper in your hand suddenly feels heavier.

You'd already imagined new floors, fresh paint, walking away from your cramped apartment.

Now this?

You grip the steering wheel. Something in you shifts. Not fear—resolve. You open the car door. You slam it shut.

Paperwork in one hand.

Authority in the other.

You walk toward the house like you own it—because you do. Each step hits harder than the last.

You didn't build it.

You didn't buy it.

But it's yours.

Legally.

You reach the front door. You hear laughter from inside—music, maybe. Trash on the porch. Someone else living in what's rightfully yours. You raise your fist and pound on the door.

The knock echoes through the halls of a house you've never been in.

And what happens next…

puts you in the middle of the fight of your life.

I know that scene better than most.

Because that's my Monday morning.

I work in estate settlement—the world where someone's signature turns into someone else's second chance. I've watched that same moment play out hundreds of times—families sitting at long tables, sorting through what was built, what was lost, and what was left behind.

Helping people claim what's rightfully theirs.

And sometimes catching myself thinking, What have I really inherited?

Let's hold that note for a second...

In this book, we've discussed global iconic figures—from presidents to pop stars.

And there's one legal process that connects all of them: estate law.

Because whether you die on a throne, on stage, or on the runway, one truth never changes—

The moment the person who wrote the will dies, the covenant takes effect.

Abraham Lincoln

Died without a will—intestate—leaving behind an estate worth about $110,000 (roughly $3 million today).

Even the president who wrote the Emancipation Proclamation didn't plan his own will.

John F. Kennedy

Had a detailed estate plan and revocable trust; his will poured all assets into that trust for Jacqueline and their children.

Even in death, JFK proved that legacy doesn't happen by accident—it's structured.

188 | ### Marilyn Monroe

Left 75 percent of her estate to acting coach Lee Strasberg—who passed it to his widow, a woman Monroe never met.

Her "brand" was later ruled public domain after a court battle revealed that her right of publicity died with her.

A global icon—legally inherited by a stranger.

Elvis Presley

When Elvis died in 1977, his estate was nearly bankrupt from mismanagement and overspending.

His daughter Lisa Marie turned Graceland into a museum, resurrecting the Presley fortune.

A blueprint for what happens when fame dies faster than finances.

Princess Diana

Her will left most possessions to William and Harry, but she also set aside seventeen personal items for her godchildren.

After her death, her family fought over letters, dresses, and gifts—proof that even royal inheritance can become common drama.

Michael Jackson

Left 40 percent to his mother, 40 percent to his kids, 20 percent to charity—and *nothing to his father.*

The King of Pop cut his dad out of the kingdom.

His estate remains in probate today, worth billions.

Lincoln. Unprepared.
Monroe. Monroe. Inherited by a total stranger.
Jackson. Protected.

Different stories—same law.

Every one of them—presidents, pop stars, pastors, prophets—faced the same courtroom principle:

When the author of the will dies, the will is activated.

Now let me take you to a real table—a real estate meeting that changed the way I see heaven's inheritance plan.

It was a quiet Sunday morning on the east coast of Florida.

The kind of morning *too peaceful to hold something so prophetic.*

The sun was climbing behind me as I drove east—toward the ocean, toward another estate, toward another meeting I almost ignored. | 189

The week before, the executor had called me several times.

To be honest, I was too busy.

Too distracted with my other businesses.

Too consumed with schedules, employees, and life.

He kept following up, but I kept brushing him off.

I didn't realize I was about to walk into a *divine appointment*—one that would unlock the *third act of my revelation.*

When I arrived at the house, it felt sacred.
Not religious.
Just…still.

Grief hung thick in the air.
Love lingered in the rooms like perfume.

Four adult siblings greeted me at the door.
Their mother had passed only weeks before.
They'd just returned from scattering her ashes.
Now they were gathered at her kitchen table—the same table where she once served them breakfast and prayed over scraped knees and teenage heartbreaks.

Now the table was covered in paperwork: legal documents, bank statements, photographs, jewelry, and a copy of her *Last Will and Testament*.

They walked me through the home, *room by room, memory by memory.*
They showed me the fine china she never used, the wedding ring she always wore, the closet full of vintage clothes untouched for years.

I listened.
I guided.
I offered professional advice.
I promised to help them honor her legacy.

But something was stirring inside me the entire time.
When I stepped out, climbed into my truck, and shut the door, I didn't start the engine.
I just sat there—because something was shifting.
And that's when a still voice whispered:

> *"This is what I did for you."*

At first, I didn't understand. Then the lightbulb went off—
and a *wave of revelation crashed over me.*
That kitchen table wasn't just a table.

It was a *mirror*.

A *prophetic picture*.

An *invitation into deeper understanding.*

God wasn't reminding me of my profession.
He was revealing the *estate plan of heaven.*

We hear about salvation. We preach grace. We quote Scripture.
But we miss *something massive.*

The *New Testament* isn't just a collection of parables or inspirational verses.
It's not cute stories or poetry.
It's a legal document.
A will.
An estate plan.

And just like *in the natural,*
a will doesn't go into effect until someone dies.

"Where a will is involved, the death of the one who made it must be established.
For a will takes effect only at death."
— Hebrews 9:16–17 ESV

That's when it hit me.
Jesus didn't just die to forgive sin.
He died to *activate the will.*

This is why the devil fights you so hard.
Not because you're going to church.
Not because you're reading devotionals or self-help books.
Not even because you're learning about faith.

He doesn't fear your knowledge.
He fears your *enforcement.*

Because the moment you realize what's in the will—
and that *your name is written in it*—
you become dangerous.

The enemy's worst nightmare isn't an emotional Christian.
It's an *informed heir.*

A son or daughter who walks into court with the document in

hand and says,

> *"This is mine, and I have the right to claim it."*

And suddenly, everything from my past started connecting:
- The haunted building, where I had the keys but something else occupied the space.
- The legal battle, where I had the contract but it was being contested.
- The courtroom fights, where I had to prove my standing to gain access to what was already mine.

All of it was more than business.
It was a *living parable.*

God was teaching me through my own life that I'd been written into a better contract, a better promise, a better covenant.
And I realized something else.

The *New Testament* wasn't just good news—
it was a binding document,
    sealed in blood,
        signed by Jesus,
            enforced by His resurrection,
and backed by all of heaven.

That round table where those four siblings sat
was a reflection of the round table we will all one day will sit at with our heavenly Father—
where our name is *already written into His plan.*
And once you know your name is there…*everything changes.*

Back to the opening scene.
    Standing in front of something that legally belongs to you, only to find squatters trespassing on what's rightfully yours—
    it happens every day.
    In the physical world.
    And in the spiritual one.

    And here's where things get crazy.
    Millions hold the legal document in their hands but have no idea

how to serve notice—how to evict the trespassers.

By this point in my journey, I had discovered *three revelations* of who God is.

Growing up, I saw God through a religious lens.

Every time I left the house, my mother wagged her finger and said, "Be careful—God is watching you."

She meant well. I cherish her faith.

But I misinterpreted it.

I imagined heaven keeping score—

a cosmic mafia boss ready to send angels to rough me up if I stepped out of line.

Religion can restrain the heart,
but it can never transform it.

Later came the second revelation: *grace.*

That's why one of my favorite verses is 2 Corinthians 12:9 ESV where Paul wrestles with weakness and hears God say,

"My grace is sufficient for you, for My power is made perfect in weakness."

In my twenties, facing my own weakness,
that verse hit like cold water in a desert.

Still, I was missing the third act—the revelation that explains who we are in Christ.

And it wasn't until that day, sitting at that table, that the puzzle came together.

God hadn't been hiding it.

Religion and pop culture had just blurred it.

Now when I see the words *New Testament* printed on my Bible,
they carry new weight.

Because when you sit in an attorney's office to finalize a will, the document is literally called a Last Will and Testament.

Two legal terms: *Will* and *Testament.*

Chapter 13 will deal with the war over the human will; this chapter reveals the legal covenant—the Testament.

I used to wonder if I'd ever be good enough.

If people knew how broken I really was.
That guilt and shame followed me from childhood into adulthood.
We learn to bury it.
To hide it.
To walk as servants—in our father's house.
Then it hit me.

When Jesus stepped onto the scene,
fasting forty days and nights in the desert,
He was hungry—physically depleted.
And that's when the devil showed up.

Because it's usually when we're empty, tired, or in need that our sonship gets tested.

"If You are the Son of God, tell these stones to become bread."
—Matthew 4:3 NIV

The Bible is intentional here—it tells us Jesus was hungry. Need has a way of revealing whether we know who we are.
The devil didn't come questioning Jesus' miracles.
Not His attendance record.

Not His debates with religious leaders.

He attacked His identity.

His sonship.

And Jesus answered him:

"It is written: 'Man shall not live on bread alone,
but on every word that comes from the mouth of God.'"
—Matthew 4:4 NIV

And what was the first thing the Father affirmed when Jesus was baptized by John?

"This is My beloved Son, in whom I am well pleased."
—Matthew 3:17 NKJV

Parents, take note.
There's power in looking your children in the eyes and saying,
"I'm proud of you."

I'm intentional about how I speak to mine.

I remind them who they are, what they carry, and that I'll always be there.

So why does the enemy work overtime to distort humanity's view of a God who calls Himself *Father*?

Maybe because when you're not seated at the kitchen table with Dad—you'll never talk about a will.

Those conversations feel too heavy—no one wants to face mortality. But that's the problem: what's *unspoken leaves heirs unprepared*.

And as I studied Scripture, I realized inheritance language is everywhere.

We are co-heirs with Christ. —Romans 8:17

We've been adopted. —Ephesians 1:5

No weapon formed against me shall prosper…

this is my heritage — my inheritance. —Isaiah 54:17 NKJV

"This cup is the new covenant in my blood." —Luke 22:20 NIV

It was all legal language—intentional, not coincidence.

I couldn't believe it.

Four decades in church, thousands of sermons,

and I'd *never grasped this:*

a Father in heaven wrote me into a will.

Families fight over wills all the time.

Parents disinherit children.

But what if most believers *don't even know they're heirs—*

that they've been handed keys and authority,

but stand outside their own property while squatters live inside?

What if the next step is to serve legal notice on hell and say,

"I'm the rightful heir of every promise my Father made"?

Because the squatter only stays as long as you stay silent.

Could this change how we pray?

How we walk into boardrooms and battlefields alike?

What if every time we saw something out of alignment with heaven, we served notice and *enforced the will*?

At first, I thought it was coincidence.
But it kept burning in me like fire in my bones.
Because in this investigation I've learned—
there are *no coincidences in God.*
He's intentional with every word, every clause, every covenant.

People often ask, "Why do some see miracles while others don't?"
I can't answer every mystery, but here's what I know:
There's a difference between a religious person who says they believe in God—and a child of God who walks in their inheritance.
I remember one Tuesday night, running sound for a small prayer service.
Half-empty sanctuary.
Faithful people, older saints, praying their hearts out.
Beautiful. Sincere.
But something felt off.

They sounded like they were *begging God to do what He'd already done.*

As a father, that scene hit me differently.
I've learned more about God from *fatherhood* than from a thousand sermons.

If my daughter walked up to me hungry and said,
"Oh Father, *please grant me permission* to open the refrigerator,"
I'd smile and say, *"Sweetheart, it's already yours."*

Imagine her coming back again and again,
pleading for what was never withheld.

That's how many believers approach prayer—
begging for access to what's already been unlocked.

Many give up too soon, sitting outside the gates of their inheritance, paperwork in hand, unsure how to enforce it.
But a good father wants his children to walk freely in his house, to enjoy both protection and provision.
So what must God feel
when we beg Him to move,

when He already said, access granted?

The moment Jesus died, when he said *"It is finished"*—
the temple veil ripped from top to bottom—
the barrier between humanity and God demolished.

We are seated with Christ in heavenly places.
Not someday. *Now.*
So yes—go to church.
Read the verses.
Study the stories.
But don't stop there.

Pick up the *will.*
Read the *clauses.*
Enforce the inheritance.
Walk into the spiritual courtroom of life with boldness and legal authority.
Because your heavenly Father didn't just *save you from something*—

He gave you a seat at the table.
He *wrote you into* God's estate plan.

Baptized in Fear

A Haunted Generation

Don't buy sleep. Receive rest.

I was somewhere between seven and twelve when the nightmares began. Not the once-in-a-while kind that comes from eating too much pizza before bed.

These were repetitive.

Chronic.

The kind that leave fingerprints on the soul.

Maybe part of it was my fault. My parents warned me not to watch scary movies, but I was drawn to them like a moth to a match. Fear fascinated me.

I can still remember waking in the night and seeing a figure in the corner—a jacket draped over the vacuum cleaner, catching the light just right to become a silhouette.

But at nine years old, the imagination doesn't negotiate.

Darkness is always alive.

I wasn't alone in that fear. Every parent knows the script: a child calling out about monsters under the bed or ghosts in the closet. Only mine were persistent—vivid nighttime terrors that came in waves. And when they came, I did the only thing a child could do when evil feels inches from the mattress, nails extended, ready to strike.

I screamed.

"Dad!"

My father was the kind of preacher people said was anointed. God's presence seemed to follow him like static on the air.

But it always amazed me that down the hallway from that anointing, there could still be fear.

Maybe some would brush it off—kids have nightmares. Others might whisper that chronic terror hints at something deeper. All I know is that when I screamed, my father always came.

Every time.

Like clockwork.

I'd hear the thud of feet hitting the floor, the quick steps crossing the hallway, and then—he was there.

Even in darkness, I could feel his presence. He'd whisper, "It's okay. I'm here."

I remember one night clearer than the rest: him kneeling beside my bed, still in his pajamas, his hand on my shoulder. The same man who powerfully spoke from pulpits to hundreds, sometimes thousands, now whispering to a frightened boy. In that moment, he wasn't Mr. Bishop of the Midwest. He wasn't Pastor Herman.

He was just—

Dad.

And when he was there, the monsters shrank to the size of ants. Peace entered the room without turning on a light. I slept like a baby.

Years later, I'm writing about a generation that can't or couldn't seem to sleep—anxious, medicated, ritual-bound. We've made rest into a performance: blue-light filters, white-noise machines, melatonin gummies, sleep-tracking apps. All of it an attempt to engineer what my father gave me for free—presence.

Rest.

Sleep.

Peace.

As I began researching this topic, new names started pinning themselves to my evidence board.

Not saints or prophets.

Pop icons.

Names everyone knows, still breathing the same air as you and me.

A guy named Abel—an international popstar—better known to the world as The Weeknd.

A famous singer named Billie Eilish.

Kendall Jenner, supermodel, influencer, face on every magazine rack.

Different worlds. Same symptom.

They can't sleep.

Not in my words—in their own.

Some have said they're terrified to close their eyes.

The Weeknd has spoken publicly about years of sleep paralysis—his villain, his curse. He built an entire film, *Hurry Up Tomorrow*, and a song, "Baptized in Fear," out of those nights when he awoke frozen, shadowy figures hovering at the edge of vision.

Billie Eilish wrote music titled "When We All Fall Asleep, Where Do We Go?" from the same well of midnight terror.

Kendall Jenner on an episode of the hit TV show *Keeping Up with the Kardashians*—confessed to battling her own sleep issues and dread.

Maybe the neurologists have charts and explanations—REM disorders, stress, bad sleep posture.

And maybe that's true sometimes. But what if sometimes there's more? What if something spiritual hums beneath the clinical noise?

That question stopped me cold.

Because these are the people the world envies—the ultra-wealthy, the admired, the adored. They can summon jets, fly anywhere, hire guards, buy peace by the acre.

And still—they can't rest.

While the average person wonders how to pay the electric bill, these global elites would probably trade millions for one decent night's sleep.

So no, this chapter isn't written to mock them. I believe every one of them carries a God-given gift, a divine spark that made them who they are.

But their sleeplessness exposes something cultural.

It's a mirror to all of us.

Because even with all our power, we still can't buy peace.

As I kept digging, I realized this mystery isn't new. For centuries, people have described the same nocturnal terror. The ancients called it the incubus or succubus—spirits pressing on the chest, stealing breath, pinning the body between worlds. Today we call it sleep paralysis.

Same darkness. New vocabulary.

I'm not here to solve the argument between theologians and neurologists.

I'm here to talk about one five-letter word—*sleep*.

Because sleep, both biologically and spiritually, is sacred ground. It's the one time every day God forces humanity to *practice trust*.

When we surrender control, He performs His quietest miracles—cell repair, memory integration, emotional reset.

It's as if He built into our biology a nightly sermon—reminding us:

You are not in charge.

And still we resist it.

What did God do on the seventh day of creation?
He rested.

Not because He was tired.
Because He was finished.

Genesis says He blessed that day and called it holy.
The Hebrew word is *Shabbat*—to cease, to stop striving.
Rest became God's signature over creation, His way of saying:

"*It's done. It's good. I reign.*"

Even Charlie Kirk, the political voice who'd built an empire of microphones and movement, talked often about that same principle. He called it Shabbat—a full stop, electronics down, family up.

A day to quit performing and start being.
He believed in rest, at least conceptually.

And then came the detail that drew my investigator's eye back to him.

Candace Owens—the friend, the commentator—went public with text messages, calling them receipts. She claimed Charlie had vivid dreams, nightmares, even a foreboding sense of death years before it happened. In her podcast, she scrolled through their old messages: April 6, 2018.

He joked about being Moses, about seeing what was coming for the nation, about maybe not living to see it through. He called it prophecy. As Candace showed the text messages on screen Charlie further wrote:

> *"If I tell you the true prophecy that I know in my gut it's really sad. But I hope it's wrong"*

In Chapter 4, I went further into detail about his specific words…
He called it gut instinct.
Either way, it was unrest.

At the time of this writing, her short clip had millions of views.
And again, this isn't about disrespect. It's about evidence. When you follow patterns, you follow them wherever they lead.
So I paused.
If her account is accurate, then Charlie, too, was losing sleep—physically, spiritually, prophetically.
And that put him on the same board as The Weeknd, Billie Eilish, and a gallery of others who can't seem to rest. People who had never shared a dinner table. Yet spiritually connected by the same symptom: sleeplessness.

And that's when the pattern sharpened.

I started seeing sleep itself not as a neutral biological rhythm but as a battlefield.
Because while Jesus slept through storms, our generation drowns in them.

While God rested after creation, we panic after completion.

While the Father watches, we stare at screens, afraid of silence. | 205

Something deeper is happening.
Something that mocks rest.
A counterfeit peace being sold at a premium.

Then came the ancient parallels: Adam's deep sleep, Abram's covenant sleep, David's enemies under divine sleep, and the Son of God asleep on a boat while seasoned fishermen screamed.
Jesus woke, rebuked the storm—and then rebuked their fear.
He wasn't angry about water in the boat.

He was grieved by fear in their hearts.

Because in Heaven's logic, rest is warfare.

When I kept digging, the pattern widened.

Sleep wasn't a side detail in Scripture—it was the hinge on which God kept turning the story.

He built a bride while Adam slept.

He cut a covenant while Abram slept.

He dropped Saul's army under a divine trance so David could walk away unharmed.

He showed Jacob a ladder to heaven in a dream.

He gave Solomon wisdom in the dark.

He warned Joseph to protect Mary and the Child while he slept.

Every major transition in the Bible happened when man stopped striving and God started moving.

Which makes you wonder: if rest is Heaven's open door, what happens when a generation can't sleep?

I started pinning names to the board—Abel (The Weeknd). Billie Eilish. Kendall Jenner. Charlie Kirk. And then another face demanded its place: **Michael Jackson**.

He had long-standing insomnia. After he died, LA County's coroner ruled the cause *"acute propofol intoxication."* Propofol—administered as a sleep aid outside a hospital setting—became the very thing that stopped his heart. Those details spilled out in open court; the physician was ultimately convicted.

I can't shake the irony.

While others around him kept hitting snooze—literally or spiritually—he couldn't seem to sleep, until the remedy he trusted to keep him down took him out.

He was trying to buy what God gives away: peace.

The pop icon who moon-walked across stadiums couldn't moonwalk his way back to peace in his own bedroom.

That isn't mockery; it's a mirror—a warning.

It proves what every sedative eventually confesses: **fake sleep can kill you.**

This is where the bigger issue in culture started to sharpen.

These weren't random headlines; they were **threads**—modern symptoms of a sleep epidemic, a spiritual crisis.

The world's sleeplessness isn't only a medical problem; it's a **cultural confession** that we've forgotten the art of spiritual rest.

As I continued studying **the record**—legal, historical, spiritual—it became obvious: sleep is never neutral. It's either **surrender** or **sedation**.

That's why, in **Genesis**, God works while man sleeps; and in **Gethsemane**, man sleeps while God works.

The holy kind of rest lets Heaven move.

The unholy kind sedates—shadowed by night terrors and baptized in anxiety.

And if we want to talk about someone who had the right to say they lost sleep the night before, we should put another name on the evidence board.

David.

Aka—King David.

Aka—the psalmist David.

This was a man who had every reason to sleep with one eye open and a hand on his sword.

And if you want to talk about spiritual warfare—someone who had more problems than just how to pay his phone bill—you focus your sights on David.

During a time when it seemed like everyone was out to get him, | 207 look what he wrote in the Bible:

"In peace I will lie down and sleep, for you alone, O Lord, make me dwell in safety."

—Psalm 4:8 NIV

That verse is David's declaration of trust replacing terror. He wrote it in a time of conflict—his enemies were plotting against him—yet he still said, *"I'm going to bed."*

Here are a few more that reinforce that same truth:
- Psalm 3:5 NKJV, "I lay down and slept; I awoke again, for the Lord sustains me."
- Proverbs 3:24 NIV, "When you lie down, you will not be afraid; when you lie down, your sleep will be sweet."
- Psalm 91:5 NIV, "You will not fear the terror of night, nor the arrow that flies by day."

"You will keep him in perfect peace, whose minds are stayed on You."
—Isaiah 26:3 NKJV

If David could sleep in a war zone, then I had to ask why I kept losing sleep in peacetime.

At this point, I began to realize there were nights in my own life when I lost sleep. I can specifically remember, in my early twenties, tossing and turning all night—my mind racing a million miles an hour.

Worried about my career. Worried about bills. Worried about investing in my companies.

Anxiety was knocking on the door, asking if it could sleep over.

Grown people don't usually scream for their fathers—
but our souls still listen for the footsteps of rescue.

I'll never forget that season of my life. Although I was a grown man by then, the nine-year-old in me still wanted to scream for my dad to run into the room. I was facing daily stress—something I'm sure you can relate to.

That reoccurring, reappearing thought that waits until midnight to visit you. That feeling that slides under the door when you should be resting. The one that steals your breath before your alarm clock even goes off. And if that's you—if you fight those shadows—then maybe, just maybe, you're haunted.

Haunted literally means to be repeatedly visited by something that no longer has authority but still occupies space.

That's what fear does. It keeps showing up in rooms where it's already been evicted.

A haunted house isn't dangerous because the walls move—it's dangerous because something refuses to leave.

And a haunted generation is one that refuses to let go—of trauma, of control, of the belief that God abandoned the hallway.

We call it anxiety.

Heaven calls it unfinished business.

When divine order breaks, spiritual echoes fill the silence.
When rest disappears, ghosts rush in to take its place.

That's why Jesus didn't just cast out demons—He restored rhythm.
He calmed storms.
He told the weary to rest.
He told the fearful to be still.
Because the cure for being haunted isn't holy water.
It's holy order.

Because here's the deal:

Fear is counterfeit faith—it believes in the wrong kingdom's promises.
And if we don't believe someone's watching the hallway of our lives, we'll always sleep with one eye open.

That's why anxiety exhausts you; it's worship in reverse, meditating on the devil's possibilities instead of God's guarantees.
Faith says, "It's done."
Fear says, "What if it's not?"

So when a generation is baptized in fear, it loses the currency of Heaven.
And if fear is a counterfeit liturgy, then culture is its cathedral.

And then I really went down the rabbit hole.
Because no wonder big conglomerates seem to cash in on the idea of scaring kids.
Now I know a little something about this topic. Growing up and being single, I could care less about what was happening in media. But once I became a father—the *tables turned*.

Fatherhood made me the usher at my home's doorway—deciding which spirits got a seat.

I wanted to get a good night's rest, and I wanted my child to get a good night's rest. Remembering how I grew up, I was determined not to allow that same villain into my home.

In my house, we don't watch scary movies.

I'm not judging you if you do—if you can handle it and still sleep tight, more power to you. However, I was deliberate about what I allowed into my home and what I allowed near my children.

The more I watched, the more I saw it: fear isn't just a theme—it's a **business model**.

And that's when I started to realize that some of these major companies that make themselves out to be kid-friendly either aren't parents themselves—the people writing the scripts—or there's some kind of hidden agenda.

Because as I would sit and watch movies with my oldest daughter when she was younger, I started to wonder why the music was always so spooky, why there was always somehow an evil witch in each story.

And I remember asking my wife, *"You've got to be kidding me. Can't they just give us wholesome entertainment without glorifying fear?"*

Because stories don't just entertain us—at night, they catechize us.

Which brings me back to not just the names of the famous people mentioned in this chapter, but to all of us.

Are we getting good sleep?

When you lay your head down at night, are you going into a peaceful rest?

Or are the worries and challenges of life succeeding at breaking our nocturnal, God-ordained rhythm?

As we look back at the patterns in this book, one of the clearest appears in Abraham Lincoln—who dreamed of his own death just ten days before the assassination. It was an eerie dream, one he even described to those around him in unsettling detail: death.

Was that evil trying to hand him a script and asking him to recite it?

Was it God—or an angel—trying to give him a warning?

Was it maybe just a neurological issue doctors could explain away—maybe too much on his mind before bed?

Still—since numbers matter to God—it's hard to ignore the number ten.

The number ten has always marked Divine order.

Ten commandments.

Ten plagues.

Ten generations from Adam to Noah, and again from Noah to Abraham.

In every case, ten represented Heaven establishing rhythm—structure—law.

It was God saying, "Here's how My world holds together."

But when that order is broken…everything trembles.

Because man was designed to live in sync with that divine calibration.

And when we step out of rhythm—when rest becomes optional instead of sacred—the consequences ripple through nations.

That's why sleep isn't trivial.

It's the signal that the system is aligned.

Heaven created day and night not just for light and darkness, but for balance between labor and trust.

When that balance is lost—when our sleep is disturbed—the human spirit drifts out of tune with its Creator.

Ten goes deeper than sleep.

It isn't a countdown to tragedy—it's an invitation back to balance.

God's divine order has always wanted one thing for all of us—peaceful rest.

Even for the names mentioned in this book.

Even for the ones who never woke up.

Because Heaven's heartbeat has never changed.

Its rhythm still whispers the same call:

"Come to me, all of you who are weary and carry heavy burdens, and I will give you rest."
—Matthew 11:28 NLT

When man loses that order, chaos multiplies.

When a generation forgets the Sabbath—to rest in the Creator—it forgets safety.

When rest is lost, revelation stops.

I'm not a conspiracy theorist, but I do believe God speaks through patterns.

And sometimes, He even speaks through numbers.

That's why it's hard to ignore what happened on September 10— the day Charlie Kirk's life was taken.

Ten has always marked divine order and human responsibility.

And yet, when order breaks, even the date itself seems to echo Heaven's grief.

So maybe that's why both Abraham Lincoln's and Charlie Kirk's stories intersected with the number ten.

Not as proof that God caused their deaths—but as a sobering sign that creation itself groans when divine order is ignored.

Ten might not have been Heaven's signature.
It might have been Heaven's siren.

Because when man falls out of rhythm with God's rest, the results can be catastrophic.

Civilizations collapse.

Empires unravel.

Even the most righteous fall asleep at the wrong time—and never wake up.

Rest is the regulator of revelation.

And every other name mentioned in Chapter 3—they all seemed to have been sleep-deprived.

Was that just a symptom of a deeper, spiritually rooted issue?

Faith?

Who you put your trust in?

And again, my sincere hope is that all these people were able to have some kind of spiritual reckoning at some point. Maybe the history books will never reveal it. Hopefully they all placed their trust in Jesus.

Because I want to be sensitive here. In a world where everyone seems to treat opinions like verdicts on social media—as though we know how every atom in our bodies was placed there, as though we understand the cosmic mysteries of the universe—I want to pause and make it clear: *only God knows the human heart.*

I'll honor that mystery—
and I'll still follow the trail.

However, you're reading this book because you trusted me to take you into this deep spiritual investigation, so I lay out the facts.

And although we can do nothing to change the past, we can **absolutely** affect the future.

So I challenge every person reading this chapter.

I challenge every celebrity terrified to turn off the lights and go to sleep at night.

I know that religion may have disappointed you. I know that people in suits or robes may have left a bad taste in your mouth regarding God—or His Son, Jesus Christ.

I'm not here to ask you to drop everything, buy a new shirt, and accompany me to Sunday school.

No. Because I believe in a Jesus who meets you **outside** the four walls of the building some mistakenly call *"the church."*

The Jesus I know is the one murdered for being called the friend of sinners—the one who sat at tables with the most haunted people of His time.

And there never was a Jesus dinner that didn't end with a radically transformed heart.

So let me show you the **receipt** of His love, written centuries before He bled.

When I was pushed away from religious events—finding myself in the sketchiest hotel rooms, doing things I wasn't proud of—I met a man with a beard. The Bible says His beard was ripped out.

Yes, in the book of Isaiah, Chapters 50, 52, and 53—what are called the Messianic prophecies—one of the most graphic descriptions in the Old Testament depicts the suffering of the Messiah, Jesus, before the crucifixion.

This may sound random, but stay with me—it connects.

Pause. Let's talk about beards.

When I was younger, I got invited to play at a major church event—thousands of people, a huge convention center, the kind you drive halfway across the country to reach. After hours on the road, hungry, sleep-deprived, and racing traffic, I finally made it to the stage.

And that's when one of the youth leaders—posted like a bouncer guarding holy ground—stopped me.

He looked me up and down, then said, "You can't play tonight."

I asked, "Why?"

He said, "Because the church bylaws state that men aren't allowed to have facial hair."

Now put yourself in my shoes.

I had just driven over fifteen hundred miles to play the piano for God—but it felt as though God was standing there with a shaver in hand, saying, "Make sure he shaves before he plays a chord."

I remember looking at the guy—I'm eighteen years old and stunned—and saying, "Didn't Jesus have a beard?"

So when I read this prophecy—it hit differently.

It says He was unrecognizable, beaten beyond human likeness, and that **His beard was pulled out.**

Let that sink in.

How do you think He looked—beaten to a pulp?

This truth is life-changing if you stop the noise long enough to visualize it:

God Himself came to Earth and allowed Himself to be beaten to a bloody pulp so you could find spiritual rest that would ultimately affect your physical rest—so you would have the authority to stand up at night and speak into the darkness; to command any evil spirit trying to torment you, just as Jesus spoke to the storm for disturbing his sleep in the boat.

214|

You were created in the likeness of the Father so that you would have the authority to speak, *"Peace, be still."*

I didn't learn this in a class. I learned it when my life was coming apart.

When I understood this truth, I wasn't sitting in the second pew of a church—I was crying in a hotel room, wondering why I couldn't sleep, wondering why I was so messed up.

And just like that nine-year-old boy screaming, *"Dad!"* and hearing footsteps down the hallway—yes, just like that—when I grew older, I realized God wanted to be my heavenly Father. That included the promise of rest and peaceful sleep.

When I understood He wasn't mad at me—even though religion tossed me out of its building—I discovered He was the kind of Shepherd willing to leave the ninety-nine to search for the one missing.

And now?

Just ask my wife.

She'll tell you that no matter where I am, I can kick my feet up and start to sleep.

My body finally remembered how to rest—

our culture, somehow, forgot.

Because when a generation doesn't believe it has a loving heavenly Father outside the bedroom door, watching the hallway—when it's baptized in fear, which is the gospel of hell—

that generation forgets peace.

And with that, I challenge every person reading this book: we don't need another story about a celebrity who drugged themselves to sleep.

You're not alone. And I challenge anyone who's tried everything and still can't sleep to reach out to us on socials. We can help. No judgments.

And maybe tonight, when the world scrolls itself to sleep, you'll hear it—the quiet sound of footsteps in the hallway.

The Father still moves toward the rooms of His children.

And when He enters, every monster becomes a memory.

Now…Rest, child. He's here.

THE GOD WHO THROWS PARTIES

Scandal at the Tree

"You prepare a table before me in the presence of my enemies."

—Psalm 23:5 NIV

I t all started at the most innocent and unthinkable place.

A school playground.

At a tree.

We had just enrolled our oldest daughter in first grade. The pandemic was finally loosening its grip, and the world was trying to remember how to breathe again. Kids were relearning friendship; parents were relearning trust.

That first morning she clung to me like a child clings to air. The principal had to coax her up the steps, and I drove away watching her cry through the rearview mirror.

I circled the block, parked, and waited—in case she needed me—because that's what fathers do when they can't let go but have to.

By day three she seemed fine—until she wasn't.

Something in her eyes had changed. Parents know.

I asked gently, "How was your day, sweetheart?"

"Fine, Daddy," she said, staring out the window.

Later she told me the story.

A group of new friends had invited her to play a game by the tree.

They told her to stand there and wait while they went to "have a conversation by the monkey bars."

She waited—believing she was included—while they giggled from a distance.

They'd made her the punch line of the day.

And that night, something inside me broke.

I'd grown up on Chicago streets where reading a person's intentions was survival. I could smell a setup from a block away. I smiled, nodded, pretended calm, but my heart was a siren.

You can call it overreaction.

But when you have children who bear your eyes and your toes, any harm to them feels like stones being thrown through your own soul.

That's when I learned the word *frenemy*.

That's when I learned first graders can be crueler than gangs—because the rocks they throw are invisible.

So I did what any investigator would do when injustice hides behind innocence:

I ran *Operation Daddy Monkey Bars*.

CODE NAME: *Scandal at the Tree*.

We handled it quietly. I wrote the teacher; she understood.

She gathered the class and spoke about kindness, inclusion, empathy.

No spectacle. No punishment. Just truth spoken gently.

A few days later my daughter came home glowing.

They'd played tag together. She'd conquered the monkey bars.

Mission accomplished.

Still, I couldn't shake the image of her—alone by that tree, wondering what she'd done wrong.

If only I could shrink myself to the size of a first grader.

If only I could step onto that playground, stand beside her, teach her how to speak up.

If I couldn't stop the cruelty, at least I could stand in it with her.

But I couldn't. I was too big. Too human. Too bound by reality. | 221

And years later, I realized that moment—my ache to enter her world—wasn't just parenting.

It was prophecy.

Because somewhere, beyond time, another Father had felt the same way.

My investigation into suffering had led me down every corridor of theology and history—kings, prophets, presidents, pop icons—and all the evidence kept pointing to one scene.

A garden.
Not walled in but overflowing.
"A river watering the garden flowed out of Eden; from there it separated into four headwaters" (Genesis 2:10 NIV).

Life didn't flow toward God there—it flowed from Him.

Revelation hit me like a flashbulb on the case board.
If rivers flowed out of Eden, then revelation doesn't trickle down from our questions—it rushes outward from His heart.

It's not something we chase upstream.
It's something that's been coming for us all along.

And in that garden stood a tree.
The Tree of the Knowledge of Good and Evil—the first crime scene in human history.

Freedom required risk.

Love required freedom.

And so evil slipped in, whispering its offer: You can be like God.
The scandal that shattered paradise didn't start in a palace or a courtroom.
It started at a tree.

Thousands of years later, I stood before my own wall of evidence—photos, strings, clippings—thread after thread tracing presidents, pop stars, prophets. Every story of tragedy and redemption seemed to loop back to that same symbol.
A tree.
And then, like a whisper that wasn't a whisper, I felt it:

"Do you want to know where I was when you needed me the most? At a tree."
The revelation detonated inside me.

Everything I'd been chasing—authority, answers, redemption—was converging on that single image.

"Do you want to know where you find help in time of trouble?
At the tree.
Where you gain authority over darkness?

At the tree.
Where heaven meets humanity face-to-face?
At the tree."

That's when it clicked. The scandal of Eden was mirrored by another scandal—the scandal of grace—played out on another tree, millennia later.

Because the same Father who watched Adam and Eve fall let His own children mock, spit at, and crucify Him on a tree.

And just like me wanting to shrink down to my daughter's size, He did what I couldn't.

God actually shrunk himself to human form.

He put on flesh.

He stepped into our playground of pain.

He stood beside us, not in theory but in person.

John's Gospel records it this way:
"In the beginning was the Word, and the Word was with God, and the Word was God...And the Word became flesh and dwelt among us, and we beheld His glory."
—John 1:1, 14 NKJV

That's courtroom language if you think about it. Eyewitness testimony. Evidence entered into record. The eternal God became Exhibit A in His own defense against evil. He didn't just issue decrees from heaven—He entered the scene, took the hit, and rewrote the verdict.

And somewhere between the tree in Eden and the tree at Calvary, the greatest party in the universe was being planned.

This moment...is worth taking our time with it...there's a big payoff.

I realized that the first time fear and shame appear in the Bible was in the garden near that tree.

"Then the eyes of both of them were opened, and they knew that they were naked; and they sewed fig leaves together and made themselves coverings" (Genesis 3:7 NKJV).

And when God called out to Adam, he replied, "I heard you in the garden, and I was afraid because I was naked; so I hid" (Genesis 3:10 NIV).

Why is this important?

Because God redeemed us—from fear and shame—with a tree.

You would think God would want nothing to do with a tree if that's exactly where humanity messed everything up. So by this point, I began to learn something important about God:

God doesn't waste pain.

God doesn't waste shame.

God doesn't even waste our fears.

God waits for us in the very same place that we messed up.

If we allow Him to—He flips our mistakes into a celebration.

Don't believe me?

Let's pull up the receipts.

Because the Bible is full of moments when God threw a celebration in the exact place people expected silence. Moments when Heaven said feast instead of funeral.

When Israel escaped Egypt, they didn't tiptoe out with trauma therapy appointments—they marched out with tambourines. Right after generations of slavery, God's first instruction wasn't "Go hide and recover," it was "Hold a feast to Me in the wilderness" (Exodus 5:1 NKJV). A festival in the desert. A party in the pain.

Or think of Purim. Haman had written the death sentence for the Jews. Gallows were built. The decree was signed. And just when everyone was sure mourning was permanent, God flipped the script—literally: "The month which was turned from sorrow to joy… and mourning into a holiday" (Esther 9:22 NKJV). They didn't just survive; they threw a nationwide block party.

224| And the Passover? It was born in a night of judgment, blood, and fear. Families huddled inside while death swept through Egypt—and God said, "This day shall be to you a memorial; and you shall keep it as a feast to the Lord" (Exodus 12:14 NKJV). A meal in the middle of chaos.

It's almost as if God insists on celebrating in the very places the enemy tried to shame us. He doesn't just erase pain; He redeems it with music and dancing.

Everywhere you look, He throws parties in impossible places.

At Mount Sinai—thunder still rumbling—He invites His people

to eat and drink in His presence (Exodus 24:9–11).

At the return from exile, Nehemiah looks at a weeping crowd and says, "Do not grieve, for the joy of the Lord is your strength" (Nehemiah 8:10 NIV). Translation: dry your tears—this is a feast day.

Because God doesn't wait for everything to be perfect to celebrate. He celebrates to make things new.

And then, just when you think the divine celebration theme was a quirk of the Old Testament…the New Testament turns the volume up.

The first miracle Jesus ever performed?

Not in a temple.

Not in a courtroom.

But at a party.

A wedding in Cana.

No sermons. No scrolls. Just joy, laughter, and empty wine jars. And when the wine ran out—the symbol of joy ran dry—He didn't lecture them. The servants filled the jars to the brim, then Jesus said, "Draw some out and take it to the master of the banquet" (John 2:8 NIV).

Water became wine. Shame became laughter.

And the story of redemption began not in a funeral procession—but on a dance floor.

The Kingdom always reveals itself at tables.

Later, when the religious elite murmured about Jesus eating with sinners, Jesus didn't correct them—He confirmed it. Because Heaven's RSVP list has always been scandalous. Tax collectors, outcasts, ex-prostitutes…people who were supposed to be outside the party found themselves at the head table.

And then came the trilogy.

Jesus told the story we can't escape—the trilogy of lost things. The shepherd with one missing sheep, the woman with one missing coin, and the father with one missing prodigal son.

I found it astonishing that in each story Jesus told, there was one recurring theme—and if you blink too fast, you'll miss it.

Every time something lost was found, the same rhythm followed:
→ Lost → Found → Party.

A shepherd leaves ninety-nine safe sheep to chase down one that wandered off. When he finds it, he hoists it over his shoulders and says, "Rejoice with me; I've found my lost sheep" (Luke 15:6 NIV).

A woman loses a single silver coin, lights a lamp, sweeps the entire house until she finds it, then calls her friends: "Rejoice with me; I've found my lost coin" (Luke 15:9 NIV).

And a father watches the road until he sees his son—dirty, broken, barefoot—limping home rehearsing an apology. But before the boy can speak, the father runs to him, throws a robe over his shoulders, slides a ring on his finger, and shouts, "Kill the fatted calf! We're throwing a party!"—Luke 15:20–24 NKJV

Heaven doesn't celebrate perfection.
Heaven celebrates return.

Because repentance isn't punishment—it's the invitation that restarts the music.

Jesus said, "There is joy in the presence of the angels of God over one sinner who repents" (Luke 15:10 NKJV).

Not a slow, awkward clap.

Not polite acknowledgment.

Joy.

The sound of Heaven erupting because somebody down here just had a turning point.

That word *repentance*—in the original Greek, *metanoia*—means a change of mind. It's when you stop believing the lie that you're too far gone and start believing the truth—the truth Jesus declared from the cross: "It is finished" (John 19:30 NKJV).

Repentance is not groveling at God's feet. It's not beating yourself up every day for how you seem to keep messing up. It's standing up again in the Father's house. It's realizing what you couldn't fix on your own was already fixed on a cross. That's called grace.

Do you know how empowering that is when you finally collide with this revelation?

Paul said, "All have sinned and fall short of the glory of God" (Romans 3:23 NKJV) and centuries earlier, Isaiah wrote, "All our righteous acts are like filthy rags" (Isaiah 64:6 NIV).

Meaning? Even on your best day, you can't perform your way into perfection. To an eternally just and perfect God, trying to earn your way in by self-help or self-discipline still falls short. In a world obsessed with five-step plans and motivational formulas, the apostle Paul's reminder cuts through the noise: the only way to God is through His Son, Jesus—and what He already accomplished on the cross for you.

It's like Christmas morning. Someone buys you the perfect gift, wraps it beautifully, and places it beneath the tree. But instead of receiving it, you keep trying to pay them back for something already purchased, already delivered, already waiting.

That's what religion does.

Grace says, stop trying to buy what's already been paid for.

So yeah, God loves parties—as we've seen.
Every time a heart turns, Heaven turns up the music.
Every time a mind changes, angels start dancing.

The very word that defines a turning point on Earth is the same word Heaven uses to define revival.
Direction changes. Minds shift. Grace wins.
Heaven has always been a party waiting for one RSVP—
yours.

Which brings me back to the tree on that elementary school playground. As a father, I couldn't let my daughter feel fear, shame, or confusion at the foot of a tree. If I could've, I would've thrown the biggest party her school had ever seen right there—at the same spot others planned her humiliation.

Any good parent would.

Right there, in the presence of the very kids who decided they wanted to be her enemies—or frenemies—I would've prepared | 227 banquet tables, hired the best band, and ordered the tallest three-tier Nutella and ice-cream cake imaginable.

Because I wanted them to see what a good father does for his child.

And that's when Scripture started colliding in my mind.

God speaks to us through the psalms of David—because David understood the heart of the Father. He wrote from both the battlefield and the banquet table, from the valley of the shadow of death and the overflow of grace.

"You prepare a table before me in the presence of my enemies."
—Psalm 23:5 NIV

Could that be why the Bible says David was a man after God's own heart? Did David understand the heart of the Father?

I realized the greatest party promoter in history is God Himself.

One tree ushered in shame, guilt, and death.

Another tree brought redemption.

The apostle Paul said it best:
"Christ has redeemed us from the curse of the law, having become a curse for us (for it is written, 'Cursed is everyone who hangs on a tree')."
—Galatians 3:13 NKJV

He took the hit.

He stood where the consequences of my actions were supposed to strike me—and let them strike Him instead.

And later, Paul doubles down:
"He made Him who knew no sin to be sin for us, that we might become the righteousness of God in Him."
—2 Corinthians 5:21 NKJV

That was the greatest exchange in history—the turning point of the universe.

He who knew no sin became sin so we could become righteous.

He lived flawless—but on that cross, He took the rap sheet of every murderer, every liar, every adulterer, every addict, every fraud. He carried crimes He never committed so the guilty could wear His innocence.

228 | It was a legal transfer.

A name-tag swap.

He put on ours—stained, torn, condemned—so He could hand us His, the one that reads Righteous.

That's what Paul meant.

Jesus wore our label so we could wear His.

And then Paul adds the courtroom detail most people miss:

"By canceling the record of debt that stood against us with its legal demands. This he set aside, nailing it to the cross."
—Colossians 2:14 ESV

Every accusation. Every failure. Every legal ordinance that condemned you—gone.
Pierced through the moment those nails hit the wood.

The cross wasn't just an execution scene.
It was a courtroom.
And your record was erased—or, in legal terms, expunged—in real time.

So yes, He became the liar.

He became the murderer.

He became every sin humanity ever authored—on the record, not in character—so that every guilty verdict could be overturned.

He did all of this…on a tree.

Instead of your name tag reading Adulterer, it now reads Righteous.
Instead of Depressed, it now reads Party Planner.
Instead of Weak, it now reads Strong.
Because Scripture says, "Let the weak say, 'I am strong" (Joel 3:10 NKJV). And Apostle Paul later echoed, "When I am weak, then I am strong" (2 Corinthians 12:10 NKJV).

All of this—every exchange, every canceled charge, every paradox—happened at the same place humanity was first targeted by the enemy:
A tree.

The place of shame became the place of celebration.
The place of death became the place of dancing.
The place of the curse became the place of the covenant.
And the cross became the ultimate turning point.
Because the story of God has always ended with a party.

And that's why the final leg of this investigation opens the last file—
It begins in Chapter 13.

And after you read it, you may never look at the number 13 the same again.

Maybe, just maybe…

The next time someone asks you,

"Where was God?"

—you tell them—

We all…nailed Him—to a tree.

And if they ask,

"Then where is He now?"

You tell them…

That's one of the craziest—and most beautiful—scandals in history.

You tell them…

Heaven has a new address.

FINAL
HOURS

SINATRA
CHRONICLE

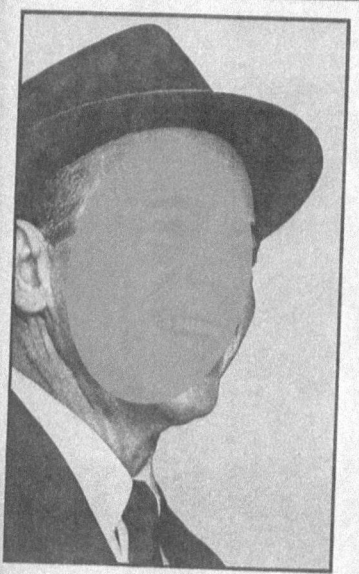

He lived on his terms
—and he died the
same way

HE
LIVED
HIS WAY

THE PEOPLE'S CHOICE

"My Way"

What if Jesus was the thirteenth—
stepping into the seat everyone else avoided?

Thirteen.

It's the number everyone whispers about.

Hotels skip it, elevators jump from twelve to fourteen, airlines renumber rows so no one sits there.

It's the number that supposedly brings bad luck.

Yet even the ancient mystics who called it "lucky" most likely knew what they were playing with.

Thirteen full moons in a year.

Thirteen—a symbol of fertility, renewal, the rhythm of nature.

Yet through history, the number 13 continued to spark terror…

But have you ever stopped to ask why? The superstition traces back centuries—some say to Friday, October 13, 1307, when King Philip IV of France ordered the mass arrest of the Knights Templar. Overnight, an entire brotherhood vanished. The Templars were accused of heresy and burned alive. Their ashes blew across Europe, and horror had a date—Friday the 13th.

And then, like most fears, Hollywood figured out how to sell it.

In 1980, the movie *Friday the 13th* dropped into theaters and forever rewired pop culture. The premise was simple: a group of teenagers on summer break, a dark lake, and a masked killer named Jason Voorhees. The film turned superstition into a cinematic ritual—every generation since has learned to flinch when the calendar lands on that date.

What used to be history turned into entertainment.

And dread became marketable.

Sequel after sequel—a generation was baptized into fear.

Now let's pause. To see what's really going on, we need to understand numbers. Now I'm not the superstitious type, but I study patterns—data and recurring themes.

As we build the *modus operandi* and a criminal profile of the one behind all of the evil we see—we have to understand fear:

Fear has always been the favorite language of the Perpetrator.

Here's the part that matters: horror is not the end goal. It's the lever. Fear is how the Perpetrator pries people loose from trust, from peace, from the voice of their Creator.

But to understand the criminal behind it—to trace his first appearance—you have to travel further back. Past the cameras and the studio lights. Past Europe's superstitions and medieval executions. All the way back to the first time the Scriptures use the word *rebellion* in history. And here are the dots we need to connect—it has to do with numbers.

Remember, if you study the story of creation in the book of Genesis, you'll see that numbers have a lot to do with God's pattern. Seven marks completion—seven days in a week, seven musical notes before the octave. Twelve marks divine order—twelve tribes, twelve apostles, twelve months in a year.

Step one number beyond twelve—just one—and you've crossed the line God Himself set in order.

Think about it: have you ever drawn a line in the sand in your life and told a friend or coworker, "You better not cross the line"?

Well, if we cross the line and go past the number 12, we step into 236| the number 13. And where do we see the number 13 mentioned for the first time in the Bible?

And what does the number 13 have to do with rebellion? Crossing the line, going past divine order, and saying I can do it on my own?

Now, before we go deeper and connect the dots, let me give you a crash course on being an investigator…

Think like a criminal profiler at CIA headquarters in Langley, VA.

Let's look at the term *Modus Operandi*.

In short, true-crime documentaries call it the "Criminal's M.O."

"Modus operandi"—Latin for method of operating—means a pattern. A signature. The tell that gives the culprit away.

Every investigator studies it. Every case depends on it.

You start with the M.O., then trace the aliases.

Aliases are the fake names and masks a criminal hides behind. Haircut, passport, accent—it changes. But the fingerprints don't.

Dust the lamp, check the doorknob, scan the window frame…and if the prints match? It's the same Perpetrator—no matter the disguise.

To understand this criminal, you have to go back further—past Hollywood, past Europe, all the way to the book of Genesis.

So we dust history.

Let's dig deeper

Something interesting happens in this biblical scene: the number thirteen is now tied to the word *rebellion*.

Let's read it:

> "And it came to pass in the days of Amraphel king of Shinar, Arioch king of Ellasar, Chedorlaomer king of Elam, and Tidal king of nations; That these made war with Bera king of Sodom, and with Birsha king of Gomorrah…Twelve years they served Chedorlaomer, and in the thirteenth year they rebelled."
> —Genesis 14:1–4 KJV

Did you catch that? The thirteenth year.

Now, as a good investigator, you'll know that the first time things are mentioned in the Bible, there's usually a reason for it.

That's the first place in Scripture where the word *rebellion* ever shows up. A coalition of kings decides they've had enough of serving another king named Chedorlaomer. So they rise up, revolt—and fall into a war they can't win.

It's the earliest recorded picture of a world trying to organize itself without God. A one-world government before the term even existed. And it ends exactly how rebellion always ends—division, destruction, confusion.

And as we follow the threat, we begin to see that it's always the same scam…

Fear whispers into their ears…

| 237

Anxiety about what may or may not happen tomorrow.
Questions like—"Did God really say that?"
That voice that keeps repeating: Where is God?
"Take matters into your own hands."

And the victim?
Begins to play that voice over and over again in their head…
What if he's right?
Well…maybe it's harmless.
"Hey, there's nothing wrong if I do this—nobody's watching anyway."

And little by little, the slow burn begins. That subtle compromise. That whisper that turns into a wildfire. The moment the victim stops running from temptation and starts negotiating with it.

Hold that pattern for a moment.

Because history has seen this movie before.

The 1960s.

The era of liberation.

War protests. Civil rights marches. Woodstock. LSD. Free love.

Two revivals rose side by side—one spiritual, one sensual.

On one side, barefoot believers strumming guitars on California beaches, launching what would be called the Jesus Movement.

On the other, flower children burning incense, chanting mantras, preaching enlightenment without repentance.

The sexual revolution had its own altar.

It didn't happen in a vacuum. The world was already on fire—Vietnam, assassinations, civil unrest. Institutions crumbled, faith in authority collapsed, and the youth went searching for meaning in every direction. Some found it in acid. Others in Scripture. Some raised their hands to Heaven; others raised their fists in protest.

The decade became a paradox—peace and protest, love and lust, revival and rebellion, all colliding on the same dance floor of history.

But zoom out. Remove the slogans. What remains?

Broken families—fatherless homes—addiction masked as intimacy—identity lost in confusion—and entertainment baptized in betrayal.

Which brings us full circle back to John Lennon from one of the most iconic bands in human history, the Beatles…

What do the Beatles have to do with the number 13?

His name is Aleister Crowley.

The phrase "the world's wickedest man" was a sensational nickname given to the English occultist and writer Aleister Crowley (1875–1947) by the mainstream press due to his controversial lifestyle and esoteric interests, including the occult, sexual liberation, and controversial drug use.

Born in 1875 in England, Crowley grew up in a strict Christian home and turned his hatred of religion into an entire philosophy of rebellion. In 1904, he wrote *The Book of the Law*, claiming it was dictated by a spirit named Aiwass. Its core command was short, seductive, and deadly:

"Do what thou wilt shall be the whole of the Law."

In other words: Do whatever you want. That's the law.

Coincidence? Maybe.

But Crowley's creed—"Do what thou wilt"—had gone mainstream.

Most of us know what it's like to follow an impulse—a feeling that seemed right at the time, only to look back with regret. Maybe it felt liberating in the moment, even justified. But later, the cost came due. That tension between impulse and wisdom isn't new; it's been the backdrop of entire generations.

Crowley later doubled down, writing that "morality is immorality in disguise."

In other words: forget right and wrong. Your will is god.

Sound familiar? That same spirit of rebellion pulsed through the 1960s counterculture—when a new generation of musicians, artists, and thinkers echoed his words without even knowing his name.

Crowley's face even appeared on The Beatles' album *Sgt. Pepper's Lonely Hearts Club Band* in 1967.

Around the same time, John Lennon famously said, "We're more | 239 popular than Jesus."

And from there, the idea spread like wildfire: Do what you want. Follow your heart. Break free from moral chains.

It felt like freedom.
But it was the oldest con in history—
dressed in tie-dye and guitar riffs.

The slogans just changed outfits:

"Follow your heart."

"Do your thing."

"Live your truth."

Catchy. Marketable. Deadly.

Now imagine walking into college orientation, sitting down, and your professor saying, "Welcome to class. Here's the curriculum, do whatever you want."

No boundaries. No accountability. No structure.

It may sound like freedom…until you realize how fast a "free-for-all" becomes a fall-for-all.

Just your will—your desire—enthroned as god.

If you were an investigator—a spiritual profiler—this is where you'd start collecting evidence. Different crime scenes. Same fingerprints.

Go back into history…

You'd find the Perpetrator's fingerprints, first in Eden, smudged across the bark of a forbidden tree.

Then at Babel, where humans tried to build Heaven out of bricks and pride.

You'd find them in Egypt, Rome, and every empire that ever rose by worshiping—self.

Fast-forward to the 20th century, and those identical fingerprints show up again—in the occult symbols stitched into album covers, the chants behind some fashion lines, the whisper in self-help books telling you to "manifest your truth."

Different aliases.

Same suspect.

He's known by many names:
The serpent in Genesis.

The dragon in Revelation.

The accuser in Job.

The father of lies in John.

But if you read between the lines, you'll see darkness taking dictation.

Crowley didn't invent rebellion—he repackaged and resold it.

In his commentary, Crowley revealed the philosophy that would become the moral soundtrack of a generation:

"There are no 'standards of Right.' Ethics is balderdash. Each Star must go its own orbit. To hell with 'moral Principle'; there is no such thing. That is a herd-delusion—and it makes men cattle."

It sounds intellectual, maybe even liberating—until you realize what's missing.

Accountability.

Design.

Truth.

It's the same lie whispered in Eden by the devil: "You can decide what's right."

"You can be your own god."

And when Jesus described the Perpetrator in plain language, He called him **"the thief."**

An expert at infiltration.

A master of disguise.

A career criminal with millennia of experience.

The thief never kicks down the door.

He waits until the lights go out.

Until the house is quiet.

Until the owner falls asleep.

Then he slips in through the window—soft, silent, surgical.

While the victim is fast asleep.

That's how culture works when it's under his influence.

He doesn't tell you to hate God; he just hums you to sleep.

A demonic lullaby—playing through playlists, streaming shows, | 241 and political slogans—each one rocking a generation further from truth.

"Do what you want."

It sounds empowering.

But it's anesthesia.

Check the footage.

The same fingerprints show up in every era.

In the corridors of power, when presidents feel doomed and paranoid—same M.O.

In studios where freedom is sold as lust and art becomes idolatry—same M.O.

In classrooms where truth is "relative" and morality is "outdated"—same M.O.

The suspect doesn't need to invent new crimes; he just rebrands old ones.

He uses different forms of identification—fear, pride, confusion, lust—but the fingerprints never change.

You can fake an ID, but not a fingerprint.

And if you lift those prints under ultraviolet light, they all trace back to the same source:

The fallen being once called Lucifer.

His co-conspirators?

The spirit of Jezebel—seduction and manipulation.

The doctrine of Balaam—compromise and greed.

The false prophet of fear—control through panic.

Together, they orchestrate humanity's favorite scam: rebellion disguised as freedom.

Now, what's fascinating is

Some sources claim the number 13 is bad luck because during the last supper in the Bible, the scene where Jesus sits with his disciples, right before Christ gets crucified, Judas, the one who betrayed him, supposedly is the 13th disciple…

Pause. Challenge that narrative…

Nowhere in the Bible does it say that.

However, in the New Testament, the connection goes to the next

level.

The number 13 now shows up again in the Bible—not as a curse, but at this dinner table.

Twelve men sit with Jesus on the night before the cross.

Twelve ordinary humans.

Then there's Him—God in flesh.

That makes thirteen.

For centuries, people said Judas was the thirteenth and that's why 13 is cursed.

But what if we've been counting wrong?

What if Jesus was the thirteenth—
stepping into the seat everyone else avoided?

He came not to join the rebellion but to redeem it.

Armed with a towel, washed His followers' feet, and sat in the "cursed" chair so He could break the curse from the inside out.

Then He went to the cross and became the curse—the ultimate undercover operation.

As we discussed back in Chapters 3 and 4, one of the world's greatest guitar players once sat at a different table in Morocco, curious and wide-eyed, as a tarot reader laid the card of death before him—number 13. Jimi Hendrix believed what he saw. He began to speak it, to own it, to live as though his fate was already sealed—that he'd die before thirty.

I can't help but wonder if anyone ever told Jimi Hendrix that he didn't have to take the card that was dealt to him. When that tarot reader laid down the thirteen of death before him and said he'd die young—he believed it. He played the hand like he had no choice.

But the truth is, the deck was already stacked against him.

That's why in the song I wrote and produced, "Where Was God," there's a line that says:

"Jimi drew thirteen, bad deck in his hand. Wish he knew
Grace still shuffled the plan."

Because that's the point—Grace was always at the table, reshuffling what hell tried to deal.

And Christ had already stepped in—He took the bad hand, the cursed seat, the losing draw—and flipped it at the cross.

So it wasn't just Jimi. It's been all of us. From Eden to now, the same lie keeps echoing through history. It seduces you into idolatry, into another bed, another distraction; then evil tries to hand humanity the death card.

That same voice that told Jimi to accept tragic fate, has been whispering to humanity since the beginning—

While rebellion screamed, "Do what you want,"

Jesus whispered, "Not My will, but Yours."

That moment flipped the entire story.

The number that symbolized rebellion now carried redemption.
The seat that once belonged to betrayal became the symbol of grace.

Pause.
We've followed the trail.
The evidence has mounted.
Now we're ready to place the suspects in a lineup—to identify the real perpetrator behind every headline and heartbreak.
The investigation leads us to this final moment…
Jesus already identified the criminal.
He told us his plan two thousand years ago:
"The thief cometh not, but for to steal, and to kill, and to destroy" (John 10:10 KJV).
But then He added the rescue clause:
"I am come that they might have life, and that they might have it more abundantly" (John 10:10 KJV).
So here we are—standing in the doorway of history's biggest crime scene.
The alarms are blaring.
The evidence is everywhere.
The same fingerprints run from Eden to Empire, from Hollywood to the headlines on your phone.
And maybe—just maybe—the thief's last disguise is convincing you that he isn't real.
But now you know better.
Now you've seen his work.
Now you've dusted the prints yourself.

THE CASE CRACKS WIDE OPEN!

The evidence jumps off the board.
Strings that stretched across the ages suddenly converge under one word: will.
Could it be that the motive was never just power, pleasure, or pride?
Could the oldest war in existence have always been a war over the definition of human will?
Because before there was a garden or a serpent or a whisper, there was an angel named Lucifer—beautiful, brilliant, created with freedom.

The same kind of freedom you and I were given. But freedom comes with risk. And Lucifer used his to speak five sentences that cracked eternity itself:

- "I will ascend into heaven,
- "I will exalt my throne above the stars of God:
- "I will sit also upon the mount of the congregation…
- "I will ascend above the heights of the clouds;
- "I will be like the most High" (Isaiah 14:13–14 KJV).

Five bullets were fired at Heaven.

Five declarations of independence.

Five times he said, "My will, not Yours."

That's the first fingerprint. That's where the M.O. begins.

Then the same voice slithered into Eden, whispering to Eve, "You shall be as gods."—Genesis 3:5 KJV

He didn't need her to hate God—just to trust her own will more.

And she did.

Centuries later, that same spirit reappears on earth, this time wearing a crown.

A man named Nimrod, the great-grandson of Noah, rises to power. Scripture says, "He was a mighty hunter before the Lord:"—Genesis 10:9 KJV, which in Hebrew can mean "in defiance of the Lord," or "we will rebel." The first organized rebellion after the Flood begins with him.

His kingdom's first city? Babel.

Nimrod stands *thirteen* generations from Adam.

Thirteen.

And just like that, the pattern takes shape.

Babel wasn't just an ancient skyscraper.

It was a movement—a global conspiracy of will. | 245

The people said, "Let us build us a city and a tower, whose top may reach unto heaven; and let us make us a name" (Genesis 11:4 KJV).

That's the heartbeat of rebellion: *Let us make our own name.*

Same crime, new century.

Same fingerprints.

The whole world was still one language, one people. No nations yet, no tribes at war. The human race had just survived the Flood. They should have remembered mercy. Instead, they built a monument to themselves. A ziggurat of defiance.

A symbol that said, We don't need God; we can reach Heaven on our own terms.

The people's choice.

And that phrase should sound familiar by now. Earlier in this book—back in the spiritual autopsy section—we saw that even the church Jesus rebuked most sharply in Revelation carried that exact idea in its name: Laodicea...*the people's choice, the people's rights*. Do you think that's a coincidence? Now... let's slip back into the story.

And God Himself came down to see it. He didn't destroy them with fire; He scattered their speech. The tower froze mid-construction, and humanity's first global rebellion fell apart in confusion. The case was temporarily closed—but the spirit of it survived.

And what drove it? Will.

The same infection that started in Heaven when Lucifer said I will ascend now surfaces in a human ruler who says, We will build.

Nimrod's tower was more than architecture; it was ideology.

It was the first declaration of human self-government against divine order—the thirteenth spirit made flesh.

Lucifer's "I will" becomes humanity's "we will."

That's the chilling connection:

The thirteenth generation from Adam embodies the thirteenth-year rebellion, both powered by the same word—will.

Twelve represents divine order. Thirteen is when we step past it.

Babel was the prototype of that overstep.

But here's where the story twists.

Most people think thirteen means bad luck. But in Hebrew, numbers aren't just digits—they carry meaning. Every letter has numeric value, and when you add them up, words themselves tell a story.

Because in Hebrew, the number thirteen doesn't mean bad luck at all. The number was hijacked—turned from a symbol of unity into one of fear.

It means love. It means oneness.

Ahavah (love) = 13
Echad (one) = 13
   (Aleph = 1 + Hey = 5 + Bet = 2 + Hey = 5 -> Total = 13)
      (Aleph = 1 + Chet = 8 + Dalet = 4 -> Total = 13)
The irony is divine.

Thirteen is what happens when Heaven and earth align—unless that extra "one" is man, not God.

Then it becomes rebellion.

The same number that represents love in Hebrew becomes the number of pride in English.

The only difference is whose will sits in that thirteenth seat.

Nimrod filled it with himself.

Christ filled it with surrender.

The board lights up again. Every red string points to the same word: *will*.

It started in Heaven with I will ascend.

It reappeared at Babel as Let us build.

Fast forward back to the 20th century—Aleister Crowley—we hear his words echoing through history…"Do what thou wilt shall be the whole of the Law."

He called it enlightenment. Heaven called it the oldest con job ever written.

Crowley even defined magic as "the Science and Art of causing Change to occur in conformity with Will."

There it is again—that obsession with bending reality to human desire.

That's Babel's tower rebuilt in print.

And today, the same creed wears new clothes:

"Follow your heart."

"Manifest your destiny."

"The will of the people."

It all sounds noble, democratic, even spiritual—but peel back the PR, and the fingerprints glow under ultraviolet light.

The same thief. The same scam. The same rebellion. |247

The case breaks.

Every crime scene we've dusted—Lucifer's fall, Babel's tower, Crowley's pen, the slogans of our age—circles the same center.

The crime isn't just disobedience. It's usurped will.

Because the enemy's dream has never changed.

He couldn't steal God's throne, so he targeted God's image instead—the human will.

He wants to twist it, repurpose it, and weaponize it against its Creator.

That's why he loves the word *freedom*. It's the perfect disguise.

He sells rebellion as liberty,

self-rule as self-care,

sin as self-expression.

And every time a human says, "My will be done," the old rebellion echoes again.

But then comes the moment that rewrites everything.

Another garden. Another night.

This time it's not Eden—it's Gethsemane.

The serpent isn't hissing; he's watching.

The Son of God kneels in the dirt, knowing he's about to face the cross, sweat turning to blood, and whispers the sentence that makes hell lose sleep:

"Not My will, but Yours, be done" (Luke 22:42 NKJV).

When you pull all those strands together—Lucifer's "I will," Nimrod's "we will," Crowley's "do what thou wilt," and Christ's "Not My will"—you begin to see the real investigation unfold.

It's the oldest cold case in the universe.

A war over will.

Not weapons. Not territory. Not even theology.

Will.

Each era simply rephrased the same confession.

Lucifer made it celestial.

Nimrod made it political.

Crowley made it mystical.

Modern culture made it fashionable.

Every generation reenacts the same rebellion with upgraded language and better lighting.

It's not superstition—it's spiritual anthropology, the science of our own rebellion.

The story of civilization is humanity rewriting the same line:

"I can decide what's good. I can define truth. I can run my own life."

That's what makes the number 13 such an important clue in our investigation.

Thirteen, the number everyone fears, was never about bad luck.

It was about alignment.

Unity when the "one" is God—rebellion when the "one" is man.

The same number that speaks of love becomes the number of pride when love turns inward.

Heaven's harmony inverted into self's soundtrack.

The paradox sits at the root of everything:

Humans.

The Tree.

Freedom.

Will.

In Eden, that tree stood as both a mirror and an invitation.

Would humanity choose trust—or curiosity without boundaries?

It wasn't fruit that doomed us—it was choice.

And ever since, we've stood between two trees:

One that promised knowledge without God.

And one that offered life through surrender.

Thirteen isn't just a number; it's a motif.

It dramatizes the moment we step past divine order or realign with it—

the line in the sand between my way and Thy way,

between Babel's bricks and Gethsemane's blood,

between illusion and intimacy,

between religion and relationship.

The Revelation stands like evidence spread across eternity's corkboard:

The fingerprints match.

Not in numerology, but in motive.

Every rebellion, every fall, every empire, every broken heart—all share the same DNA:

a will that wanted its own name more than His.

And that's when I realized— this isn't just theology. It's personal.

Because rebellion doesn't always wear horns and carry a pitchfork.

Sometimes it wears a tuxedo, holds a microphone, and croons into the smoke-filled air of a Vegas lounge.

The same era that gave us Marilyn Monroe's smile and America's golden age of glamour also gave us an anthem of autonomy—"*My Way.*"

Frank Sinatra didn't write it; it began as a French song, "*Comme d'habitude*" ("As Usual"). Paul Anka heard it in a café, bought the rights, and rewrote the lyrics overnight for Sinatra, who was pondering retirement. By 1969, it became his signature—his farewell to the world.

He stood center stage as the orchestra rose behind him, voice steady, eyes, heavy. The melody was smooth, the orchestra grand, the words deceptively noble. He sang about a man facing the end—about standing tall, refusing regret—about doing it his way.

But listen closely and you'll hear *ancient* Babel humming beneath the brass.

It became the soundtrack for funerals, weddings, and victory parties alike—an anthem of independence that made rebellion sound like romance.

People raised glasses to it, never realizing they were toasting Lucifer's oldest lyric: **I did it my way.**

The irony didn't spare its creators.

Claude François, the French singer who co-wrote "Comme d'habitude"—the song that would become "*My Way*"—died in 1978 at age 39. The story is strange but true: he was electrocuted while adjusting a light fixture above his bathtub. The man who penned the melody of self-determination died trying to fix his own light.

Elvis Presley would sing "*My Way*" toward the very end of his life. His final concert took place on June 26, 1977. When the CBS television special *Elvis in Concert* aired posthumously on October 3, the world watched him—weary, swollen, trembling—deliver the song like a prophecy fulfilled. He had recorded it only weeks before his death on August 16, 1977.

He began softly, singing the lyric stating that the *end* was *near.*

The orchestra swelled.

It wasn't a concert anymore.

It was testimony.

Not the applause of a crowd, but the confession of a soul—standing in its own defense before the Judge of the living and the dead.

Every lyric felt like a deposition.
And then came the final line—

almost legal in tone,

as if Heaven's recorder were taking it down word for word.

It sounded like a man delivering his last words, admitting that he'd absorbed every blow and lived by the choices he claimed as his own.

The courtroom seemed to fall silent.

I wonder if Elvis knew he didn't have to take the blows.

I wonder if he knew that God Himself had already taken the hit.

For a moment, imagine the room empty, the orchestra silent, the spotlight on a man whose final confession is sung in trembling vibrato. The French songwriter. The King of Rock. All of them—icons, symbols, numbers in a pattern—but more than that: real souls. People who somehow believed that doing things their way would bring freedom, joy, ultimate satisfaction.

Have you ever chased after something, ignoring that there might be a God with a plan for your life, only to discover that the light at the end of the tunnel never came? That no amount of applause, money, or control could fill the emptiness inside?

One of the wisest men who ever lived, thought to be the richest of his age, gave it words we still echo today:

"I have seen all the things that are done under the sun; and indeed, all is vanity, and a chasing after the wind." —Ecclesiastes 1:14

"Chasing the wind." That's the phrase that stops you. Wealth, fame, pleasure—they all promise satisfaction, but none deliver. They're fleeting. Hollow. Dead ends dressed as destiny.

And then I began to see the contrast, sharp as a double-edged sword: some people keep running after their way, following the melody of pride, rebellion, and impulse. Others find rest for their soul when they finally turn to a man named Jesus of Nazareth, the one who said:

"I am the way, the truth, and the life. No one comes to the Father except through me." —John 14:6

So I asked myself—what separates the ones who chase the wind from the ones who find the way? What keeps humanity from the love of the Heavenly Father, from the truth and rest that Jesus offers?

Could it be the same ancient whisper that has echoed since Eden? The one that convinces humanity to ignore the warning label on the tree of the knowledge of good and evil? To step over the line, into the thirteenth seat, thinking freedom is theirs to take?

Pause here. Let that sink in. Because right after this moment—the point where history, culture, and our own choices collide—we see the pattern again. And it leads to a single, chilling lyric:

"Do it your way."

Tragedy doesn't need a new soundtrack.

It just keeps changing genres.

Even Sinatra, surrounded by the Rat Pack—Dean Martin, Sammy Davis Jr., Peter Lawford—stood in that glamorous echo chamber of laughter and loneliness.

They were kings of cool, princes of rebellion.

And orbiting that same world? Actress Marilyn Monroe—the brightest star, burning too fast to last.

It was the soundtrack of an age convinced that the will of man was the highest law.

My way.

And maybe that's why the story that follows has stayed with me.

252 | It didn't happen in a single altar call. It was years of wrestling and prayer; of choosing—sometimes through gritted teeth—to see my father not as the man who failed me, but as a man who needed grace as desperately as I did. That's what scandalous love does. It breaks the spell of "my way," and teaches your heart to forgive even before you feel like it.

Years later, I sat at another funeral—this one personal.

My grandmother's.

The same woman who had abandoned my father when he was seven.

I didn't know her well; I'd seen her maybe four times in my life.

But I knew her shadow—the silence she left behind in my father's eyes.

By then, he was a respected pastor, a police chaplain, the kind of man who prayed with strangers in parking lots.

Yet behind the collar was still the boy who wondered why.

At the service, he stood behind a wooden podium, hands trembling, voice steady, delivering the eulogy for the woman who had walked out on him as a child.

Two hundred people filled the room—memories colliding with grief.

He spoke gently. Mercifully.

I sat there thinking, I don't know if I could have done that.

Then the music began.

Of all songs, the one that filled the room was Frank Sinatra's "*My Way.*"

They said it was her favorite.

As those famous words echoed of how he faced it all, stood tall, and did things his way, something holy fell over the room.

Not the kind of holiness that makes you raise your hands, but the kind that makes you bow your head in awe.

The scent of lilies and aftershave hung in the air.

There lay a woman who had done it her way.

And there stood a son, forgiving her anyway.

The song that once glorified independence now played as the soundtrack of loss.

And in that moment, I saw it—the holiness of choice.

The sacred paradox of freedom.

My father, the boy left behind, chose mercy over memory.

He chose surrender over bitterness.

He broke the cycle of will with grace.

That's when it all clicked.

The war over human will isn't just celestial—it's generational. | 253

It shows up at funerals, in marriages, in quiet moments where forgiveness costs more than revenge.

The real battlefield isn't Heaven or hell—it's the human heart.

So as this chapter closes, it does so not merely in theology but in testimony.

We've traced the investigation, dusted the fingerprints of rebellion across history.

But at the end of every case file lies a choice.

A choice about how you treat your family.

A choice about who you'll forgive.

A choice about whether you'll worship your own will—or surrender it.

A choice about whether you'll "do it your way" or say "Not my will, but Yours."

A choice if you'll align your words with fear—or with faith.

A choice if you'll join a powerful Church that tears down the gates of hell and speaks life into the darkness—or settle for the comfort of a lukewarm one that sleeps through the sirens.

A choice to examine the evidence and reach your own verdict:
Did they have to die the way they did?
Or could they have lived—to declare the works of the Lord?
You may have asked,
"Where was God in all of this?"
And maybe Heaven's reply is just as piercing:
"Where were you—My Church?"
And whether you're a fan or a critic of anyone named in this book, the truth remains:
You still have to face the same burning questions.

Is Heaven real?
Is evil real?
Is God real?

What could possibly change a person so completely—that they'd risk their reputation, their comfort, even their life—just to tell you about it?

What kind of encounter makes imperfect people unashamed to share their testimony?

That's the evidence you can't ignore.

Thirteen years ago, I was convinced God had written me off.

The truth is, I had questions—the same questions you have.

After the crisis. After the doors closed. After the dreams fell apart right in front of me. After businesses were lost. After the money disappeared. After the future I thought I was building collapsed like a cheap stage prop. On the outside, it looked like failure. On the inside, it felt like something darker. Something unseen. Like I was caught in a kind of spiritual crossfire I didn't yet have language for.

I ended up in a trailer park—trying to disappear, trying to breathe, trying to think. And here's the strange part: that trailer park sat directly behind a Christian broadcasting company and a Christian library. I didn't plan that. I just landed there. Or maybe I was placed there.

For months, I walked alone. I argued with God, with myself, with the mirror. I took inventory of my life and didn't like what I saw. It felt like I was standing at the foot of a tree—embarrassed, exposed, knowing I had eaten the forbidden fruit and pretending I hadn't.

One afternoon, with nothing else to do and nothing left to lose, I walked into that Christian library and spent some of my last few dollar bills on a book. Thirteen years later, the photo of me holding that book is in the photo gallery of this very book. At the time, I was looking for answers. I was looking for proof God hadn't walked away from me.

And that's when it happened.

The turning point of my entire life did not come in a church service. It did not come at an altar. It did not come through a prophetic word.

It came through a chicken sandwich.

I walked into a Wendy's at rock bottom—emotionally bankrupt, spiritually tired, trying to buy food with dignity and realizing I didn't even have enough money for that. I stood there counting coins. Short on cash. Embarrassed. Invisible. And walking back to my car, something inside me finally broke.

I asked one of the most haunting questions a human can ask: Where was God? Or worse—was He even real?

That question launched a thirteen-year investigation that took me to two trees.

The first tree—the tree of the knowledge of good and evil— where humanity chose its own way and fell. The second—the Cross of Calvary—where God Himself entered history, shrank Himself to human size, let His own creation mock Him, spit on Him, and murder Him… nailing Him to a tree.

Why would a God who could simply erase humanity instead choose to suffer for it?

That single question rearranged everything.

Galatians 3:13 says it without flinching:

"Christ hath redeemed us from the curse of the law, being made a curse for us: for it is written, Cursed is every one that hangeth on a tree."

That's where God was. Not absent. Not silent. Not distant. He was taking the curse. Absorbing the blows. Standing in the place I deserved to stand. And I didn't understand any of that at Wendy's. All I knew was that I couldn't go on pretending God didn't exist anymore.

Thirteen years later—only after finishing this book—I discovered something that wrecked me all over again. I went back to Facebook. I found the photo of me holding that book. And I realized it had been exactly thirteen years.

That's when it hit me: God had been leaving fingerprints long before I ever started looking for them.

Just like I once worked behind the scenes as a father, quietly making provision for my own daughter during her painful moment by a tree, God had been doing the same for me. Every season. Every collapse. Every detour. Every "unanswered prayer".

The God of the universe wanted a relationship with me. The God of the universe signed me into the family estate plan. The inheritance was waiting—even when I wasn't. It didn't happen overnight. It happened slowly. Relentlessly. Patiently.

And maybe that's where you find yourself right now.

Religion let you down. People let you down. Words were spoken over you that still feel like prison bars. You learned how to survive in a spiritual jail cell and started calling it normal. You've been questioning the tragedies—the headlines flooding the news cycle. And maybe, underneath it all, you're starting to feel hopeless.

But what if I told you the curse has already been broken?

That the Creator Himself spoke the three most powerful words ever uttered into existence while nailed to a tree—

'It is finished.'

The debt was settled. The sentence was carried out. The case was closed.

And yet—based on the evidence of this investigation—it didn't stop at the cross.

God didn't just cancel the curse.

He chose to take up residence inside human vessels.

If you accept the mission, your body becomes the temple of the Holy Spirit.

If you receive the truth, that truth doesn't just forgive you—it frees you.

So here's the real question:

What are the implications of a God who doesn't just save you... but moves in?

How would it shape your choices—your courage, your obedience—if you truly believed, "Greater is He who lives in you than he who is in the world"?

Because when your life aligns with Heaven's will, you don't just survive the darkness—you become a threat to it.

So wait... God's plan was not only to rescue you—but to dwell within you?

Not to shrink Himself in weakness, but to multiply His power through willing vessels?

Then we have to ask the harder question:

Why such a scandal?

Why does this idea unsettle so many religious systems—a God who doesn't just rule from a distance, but chooses to live inside His creation?

Is that where God truly is now?

Or at least... is that where He has always wanted to be?

Based on the evidence of this investigation, I have no other conclusion left to reach: humanity is caught in the middle of a cosmic war between good and evil—and at the center of it is human will.

The thief still moves—quiet, clever, practiced—slipping through culture, playlists, ideologies, whispering the same ancient lie: Do what you want—attempting at all costs—to frame God for your pain.

But now the lights are on. The evidence glows under ultraviolet grace. The fingerprints are unmistakable. You've seen the patterns. You've seen the victims. You've seen the blessings stolen and the curses recycled.

And you've been given a choice.

Christianity stands alone in this. Only one faith dares to claim that the Creator allowed Himself to be killed by His own creation to redeem that creation. No other religion spills the blood of God as evidence.

And here's the truth I learned after thirteen years in the wilderness: God is still in the business of rescuing sketchy, broken, double-life humans like me. Like you. Like all of us.

So now it's your move.

The thief isn't hiding anymore. He's in the house.

The alarm is blaring.
Will you wake up—
or hit snooze on eternity?

THIRTEEN — EXTENDED

Case File #13B : Subject—You

Classification: Active
        Status: Incomplete

You've seen the files.

You've studied the names—JFK. Marilyn. Myles Munroe. Princess Diana. Tupac. Michael Jackson. Job. And Charlie Kirk.

You've traced the patterns.

The premonitions.

The confessions.

The tarot readings.

The curses.

The last-minute words.

You've seen what happens when freedom, unmoored from its Maker, collides with human frailty—

when silence meets spiritual warfare,

when the serpent whispers…and no one answers.

You've seen the documents.

The trees.

The warnings.

The blood.

But one file remains unopened.

CASE FILE: SUBJECT YOU.

Because the real point of this investigation was never just a political or pop icon you've never met. It was never just about the headlines. It was about the mirror—

the person looking back from the page.
You.

You may have picked up this book as a seeker looking for answers.
As a fan.
As a critic.
As someone who shares Charlie's theology—or someone who rejects it.
Maybe you've never had a magazine boast about hiring witches to curse you. But maybe someone you loved spoke death over you instead of life—
death over your dreams,
death over your future.
Maybe the whisper you hear at night isn't from a headline;
maybe it's from a memory,
a parent,
a teacher,
an ex,
a doctrine that left you powerless.
Maybe it comes as a whisper…maybe as a premonition of some dark future event.
You feel helpless.
You feel hopeless.

Based on the evidence—the paper trail of history—you're not standing alone next to a tree.
Evil might think it can script your ending. But you have the freedom to rip up that script.
And as you read these pages, you start to notice something: all the breadcrumbs, all the dots, all the evidence—lead back to you.
And if you're still breathing, you have words that need to be spoken.

Regardless of your worldview, we can at least agree:
Words are powerful.
They don't just describe reality—they shape it.
They don't just fill space—they build worlds.
Jesus Himself said you'll be acquitted—or condemned—by your own words (Matthew 12:37).

Out of all living creatures, only you were made in the image of God with the power to speak words that shape destinies.

You've been given freedom. Freedom to tear up the evil story you've been rehearsing and pick up the script your Maker wrote for you.

It goes something like this:

"And we know that in all things God works for the good of those who love him, who have been called according to His purpose…What, then, shall we say in response to these things?

If God is for us, who can be against us?" —Romans 8:28, 31 NIV

So the question for you:
Will you speak blessings over yourself, your family, your circle?
Or will you align with curses and evil stories?
Even if you sense a premonition of something bad—will you just live with it?
Or will you do what God told you to do—condemn evil words?

"No weapon formed against you shall prosper, and every tongue which rises against you in judgment you shall condemn." —Isaiah 54:17 NKJV

That's your legal precedent.
Now here's the legal clause that empowers it.

"For the weapons of our warfare are not carnal but mighty in God for pulling down strongholds, casting down arguments and every high thing that exalts itself against the knowledge of God, bringing every thought into captivity to the obedience of Christ." —2 Corinthians 10:4-5 NKJV

It declares that:
- our "legal weapons" are spiritual,
- we demolish false scripts ("imaginations"), and
- we make every rogue thought submit to our inheritance clause.

Will you call the wrecking ball of Heaven to demolish every bad imagination—every evil word spoken against you?
Replace those words with His words:
"I shall not die, but live, and declare the works of the Lord."
—Psalm 118:17 NKJV

Whether you're Protestant, Catholic, atheist, or "spiritual but not religious," the case file leads back to you.

Because history—and the future—both testify:

Jesus brings an indictment against lukewarmness.

Are you on fire for God? Or have you drifted cold without realizing it? Are you sitting at His table, or pacing between two beds—like the woman seduced in aisle 4—torn between spiritual adultery and covenant?

You have an opportunity to cut the red tape.

Jesus is knocking at your door.

Will you open it?

Will you sit and have dinner with your Creator?

The case file points you to a tree.

Adam and Eve opened Pandora's box by ignoring the Manufacturer's warning label.

The serpent laughed.

But before the fruit, before the tree, before the fall—God had already written the Cross into the story. He planted that tree knowing He would take its curse.

Maybe you feel too guilty.

Too ashamed.

Too damaged.

Unqualified to speak against darkness.

I get it. I felt that way in the haunted hospital.

I froze.

I hesitated.

But that hesitation—that fear—wasn't humility. It was spiritual deception.

It was the same serpent's whisper, recycled again:

"You're not worthy."

"You're not ready."

"You don't have what it takes."

Lies.

Because here is the truth—

the same truth that sets you free.

The Infinitely Just Being—the Lawgiver of Creation—who wrote the moral law stepped off the bench,

removed His robe,

ordered Himself arrested,

and took the punishment meant for you.

Then He opened your cell,
handed you legal documents,

adopted you,

named you in His will,

and took your punishment.

"For the wages of sin is death; but the gift of God is eternal life through Jesus Christ our Lord." —Romans 6:23 NKJV

"God made Him who had no sin to be sin for us, so that in him we might become the righteousness of God." —2 Corinthians 5:21 NIV

Take a moment to absorb that.
Your fears don't scare Him.
Your mistakes don't shock Him.
He nailed them to the tree—
and left the receipt in the shape of an empty tomb.

Now you—yes, you—have been empowered, like the hero in your favorite story, who finally realizes the power that's been inside them all along.
"Now to Him who is able to do immeasurably more than all we ask or imagine, according to **His power that is at work within us…**" —Ephesians 3:20–21 (NIV)

So what now?
Will you accept the inheritance—
the authority—
the freedom documents that already bear your name?
Or will you stay in the jail cell, rehearsing someone else's script?
Because this investigation is done.
Other case files have been closed.

But yours?
Yours remains open.

Heaven is watching.

The stakes are high.

The air is heavy.

And the room has gone silent.

And now—
I'm sliding the microphone across the table to you.
You've got the mic.
Court is in session.
You're one of two witnesses left.
Heaven is holding its breath.
Your next words will be weighed, recorded, and echoed beyond this moment.
Choose them carefully.
They will be consequential.

Because this ancient enemy's playbook is always the same—
but if you belong to Jesus Christ, you win.

"He shall speak great words against the Most High, and shall wear out the saints of the Most High." —Daniel 7:25 KJV

"And they overcame him by the blood of the Lamb and by the word of their testimony." —Revelation 12:11 NKJV

Are you feeling that?

The weight of every life, every choice, every shadow colliding with the light… it's real.

All the premonitions. All the voices. All the chaos. None of it escapes the truth.

This wasn't judgment. It was an investigation. A spiritual autopsy into what was, what is, and what's to come…

Into our culture. And the invisible war behind it.

And now it's here. In your hands.

God gave you freedom. Freedom to choose…

"This day I call the heavens and the earth as witnesses against you, that I have set before you life and death, blessings and curses. Now choose life, so that you and your children may live." —Deuteronomy 30:19 NIV

Now that we know where God was… and where He wants to be…

The future looks bright.

THE MISSING WITNESS

Closing Argument

T he investigation has led us here—to a courtroom.

The more we trace the patterns, the clearer it becomes: the Bible is built on courtroom language—for a reason.
There is a Judge—God the Father, ultimate authority.

A Defense Counsel—Jesus the Son, "our Advocate with the Father." Aka our Mediator (1 John 2:1).

And a Witness—the Holy Spirit, "He will testify of Me" (John 15:26).

The jury is humanity itself, deciding whether to believe the testimony.

Jesus promised that when the Counselor came, He would testify— He would bring evidence to the stand. The Spirit's job description was never silence; it was testimony. He is the *martys*—the witness—not a martyr condemned to die, but the crucial voice whose evidence changes the verdict.

And yet, as we saw in "The Martyr We Missed," the modern world keeps repeating the same linguistic and spiritual mistake. Everywhere—on television, podcasts, memorials—people use martyr as if it means a guaranteed death.

But the word never meant death.

It meant witness—a living witness whose testimony swings the case.

A martyr was a truth-teller, not a corpse.

Death entered the picture only because some witnesses refused to recant—change their testimony—not because dying was the definition.

The word martyr—was re-wired—and when language shifts, theology follows.

Let me be clear: I am not saying any individual in these pages failed to walk with the Holy Spirit.

From the first page I've said this case is bigger than one man, one institution, or one era. But if I'm going to take readers through an investigation, then wherever the evidence leads—no matter how uncomfortable—we will go there.

Because that's what a good investigator does.

And there's no possible way to conduct a thorough investigation or present evidence at trial without the key Witness.

No court could.

And yet that's exactly what some churches have tried to do for two millennia.

They try to put on a trial—ask hearts to make the verdict—without ever presenting the key Witness.

Every courtroom thriller has its twist: the false witness.

Looks legitimate. Swears the oath. Sounds credible—then gives false testimony.

Scripture warns us: "Test the spirits to see whether they are from God" (1 John 4:1 NIV). There is a counterfeit spirit—an imitator who dresses up as light (2 Cor 11:14) and takes the stand, offering words that almost sound divine.

Could that impostor be behind some of the eerie premonitions we studied?

Maybe. Only God knows the heart.

But if even a few "revelations" came from a false witness—a voice with a stolen identity—then some people may have aligned themselves, unknowingly, with a verdict written by the wrong spirit. | 269

A forged deposition disguised as prophecy.

> *And once that testimony was accepted into evidence, the jury—the human will—reached a decision it believed was fate.*

That is not condemnation; it is a warning about spiritual chain of custody.

Any courtroom that seats a counterfeit corrupts the case.

And any church that confuses emotional energy or superstition with the Holy Spirit's voice risks coming to the same wrong verdict.

Jesus said the Spirit would testify of Him. That means the Holy Spirit was appointed to bring forward Exhibit A: Christ in us, the hope of glory (Colossians 1:27).

But instead of calling Him to the stand, religion turned Him into an exhibit—something to be observed, not heard.

We reduced the Spirit to a sensation.
Goosebumps. A shiver during a chorus.
Yes, His presence can be felt—but His assignment is far larger.
In Acts 16 the Spirit forbade Paul and his team to enter Asia—He gave strategic warnings and stops. In Acts 13 He spoke to prophets and teachers and sent workers—He gave direction. In John 16:8—Jesus said the Spirit convicts the world of sin, righteousness, and judgment—He gives discernment.
That's not goosebumps; that's governance.

He is the same person that a desperate mother—Joyce Smith once called out to in a hospital room—"Holy Spirit, please come and bring me back my son."

He is the voice that warns, Don't go, and the power that says, Speak now.
This is why Jesus ordered His disciples: Do nothing until He comes.
No sermons. No events. No strategies. *Wait for the Spirit.*

Because without the Witness, there's no evidence.
And without evidence, the world's verdict on Christ remains "unproven."

For two thousand years, man-made religion has filed paperwork—aka courtroom motions to silence the Spirit.
Fear labeled Him emotionalism.
Pride called Him disorder.
Institutions decided they could represent the case without the actual Witness.
But every generation that sidelines the Spirit repeats the same procedural error:
we put Truth on trial while the key Witness waits in the hallway.

He isn't hiding in a safe house; He's standing outside the courtroom, ready to testify. He alone carries the authentic documentation—the living evidence of Christ within.

The question is whether we will open the door and seat Him where He belongs.

Jesus also said, "You will receive power when the Holy Spirit comes on you; and you will be my witnesses" (Acts 1:8 NIV). A witness empowered by another Witness—that's heaven's strategy: authority through partnership.

When those two voices align, the case is unstoppable.

But if the Church listens to a counterfeit witness—a spirit of fear, fatalism, or fake prophecy—we authorize false testimony and nullify our own case.

"Do not quench the Spirit. Do not despise prophecies, but test everything" (1 Thessalonians 5:19-21 ESV).

That's the courtroom protocol.

Admit evidence. Cross-examine every spirit.

Truth survives scrutiny; deception demands silence.

If we believe our Father in heaven has good plans for us (Jer. 29:11)—and we refuse the lie that He orchestrates tragedy—then the drumbeat of tragedy suggests something else:

a counterfeit witness has been giving false testimony while a silent church let it stand unchallenged.

I don't know the hearts of the people mentioned in this book. Only God does.

It's not about them—It's about us now.

But the evidence forces a hard question:

Have we locked out the real Witness and let an imitator take the stand?

And as you close this book, if you're honestly searching for truth, maybe do the one thing left for any juror who's still undecided:

ask the Missing Witness—

to take the stand—and to testify. The truth, the whole truth, and nothing but the truth.

ONE MORE CLUE

Bible Prophecy / Eschatology — Mini Bible Study

You didn't choose Chapter 13.

Chapter 13 chose you.

The reveal is much bigger than you or I ever thought when we started this investigation together.

At this point in the investigation, after I pinned the number 13 to my evidence board, I realized that there was something here much bigger than me choosing to end my book on Chapter 13 for all the reasons I had previously discussed. I began to realize—after much prayer and time with God—that something far larger was at play. I felt the nudge, the prompting, the undeniable urge to reopen my Bible one last time, right before sending this book off to print.

So I did.

I opened my Bible to the book of Revelation, Chapter 13.

And that's when it happened.

Once again, I felt the unmistakable confirmation that God had taken over the investigation by this point—and He was showing me another clue.

As we know, the book of Revelation is the last book of the Bible. It's that book. The one no one really wants to crack open. Some people believe it's all a scary metaphor. Many others believe it is literal prophecy. Some believe it's a combination of both. But at the end of the day, it's an ancient text, and I wanted to search for myself.

What I realized was—the book of Revelation is not a horror story about the end of the world.

It is a love story about the end of evil.

The book of Revelation was written by John—some believe he was the same disciple who once leaned against Jesus' chest at the Last Supper.

Revelation 13 is the pivot point of the apocalypse. Arguably the most pivotal chapter in the Bible for understanding end-time human choice. When we look at Revelation Chapter 13, it becomes clear that this is the chapter where all choices collapse into one final decision.

Not philosophy.

Not symbolism alone.

Not metaphor.

Allegiance.

In the prior chapter, you might have thought to yourself, "Come on, Stevie—that's a far stretch, trying to connect the number 13 and rebellion to good old Frank Sinatra, aka Mr. 'Ol' Blue Eyes.'" But if you stick with me a little longer, you might just see what I saw—what stopped me in my tracks. Because by this point in the investigation, I thought I had closed the case file.

But then it felt like God was telling me: You're not done. There's more.

So let's look deeper.

Revelation 13 is literally my way versus His way. We already established that in this book. But if you're interested in how the story ends—when it comes to Bible prophecy and the end of the world— it's clear the Bible does not stay silent about what comes next in our culture or in the invisible war happening behind the scenes.

Now, before we dive into this powerful revelation, it's worth noting this.

As I sat there staring at the number 13 on my evidence board, I thought it only had to do with a tarot card that Jimi Hendrix may have been handed… or the connection between Adam and Nimrod, thirteen generations apart… or rebellion itself… or even the soundtrack that was played at my grandmother's funeral—the woman who abandoned my father when he was seven years old, a wound that may have rippled through our family for generations… until we stopped it.

But then I realized—it was far bigger than that.

To be fair, not everyone is skeptical of the number 13.

For some, it's unlucky. They avoid it at all costs.

But those people aren't Taylor Swift.

The superstar singer doesn't just tolerate the number—she embraces it. I once watched an interview between Taylor Swift and Jay Leno back in 2009, where she explained how deeply connected she felt to the number 13. She shared that she was born on the 13th, then turned 13 on Friday the 13th. I thought, Okay... interesting coincidence. But she didn't stop there.

She went on to explain that whenever she won a major award, she often found herself seated in the 13th row or the 13th seat. She said that whenever the number 13 showed up in her life, it brought good things.

Now before anyone jumps to accuse me of numerology or conspiracy theories, I'm simply showing you the full investigation—how these patterns surface in pop culture, in icons of our time, and in the music that shapes entire generations. It is even rumored from strong sources that Taylor Swift and her fiancé plan to set their wedding date on June 13 in 2026—or another date tied to 13. In my heart—I believe God has been showing her—all along—how much He loves her. That we all have a choice to make. The Church should stop throwing stones. We should reach the world with God's pure message of love—by starting with the truth.

So yes—13 is an ultimate paradox.

Just like the tree in the Garden of Eden.

Just like freedom itself.

Good and evil on the same branch.

Life and death in the same choice.

A paradox.

But now... back to the spiritual revelation.

If you've ever wanted to understand eschatology—which comes from the Greek word meaning the study of last things—you're in the right place.

In the prior chapter, The Spiritual autopsy, we connected the patterns between Jezebel and Balaam. But Ahat if I told you they were not the end of the story? What if they were simply setting the stage for something much larger?

You can take notes. You can open your Bible. Or you can follow along right here—I'll give you the verses and break it all down.

Let's say it plainly.

Revelation is the last showdown.

The final curtain.

The moment where God gives humanity a brief glimpse into where everything is headed.

The early chapters of Revelation expose the lukewarm church. They reveal Jezebel's seduction, Balaam's compromise, and the blending of truth with idolatry. And many believe this has already begun in our culture. Others believe it is still coming.

But then we move forward.

Revelation Chapter 12 makes it clear—the war begins in heaven.

Revelation Chapter 13 reveals something even more chilling:

The war becomes a consumer choice on earth.

In Revelation 13, Satan stops hiding.

No more subtle serpent in a garden.

No more whisper in the dark.

Now it's:

Worship or starve.

Bow or be locked out.

Take the mark or die.

That's not my language—that's the Bible's.

You want to talk about free will?

You want to talk about freedom—the very theme woven throughout this book?

In Revelation 13, free will comes under threat.

This is spiritual slavery packaged and sold as freedom.

Choice is no longer just a theme.

It becomes the thesis of the end of the world.

And what's astonishing is that the same month this book released, the man who wrote the song "*My Way*," Paul Anka, released his worldwide documentary and launched his international tour—titled

"His Way."

I wish I could tell you I planned that.

I didn't.

I don't even know the man.

And that's when I realized something unsettling.

Even though I thought I was in control of this investigation the whole time, it became clear that God had been guiding it all along—quietly, deliberately, intentionally.

And that brings us back to the anthem of choice.

"MY WAY."

That song is not nostalgia.

It is not romance.

In my opinion, it is Revelation 13 put to music.

No disrespect to its author—I believe he is immensely gifted. But the message is unmistakable.

Isaiah 14 doesn't give us poetry.

It gives us Lucifer's manifesto:

I will ascend.

I will exalt my throne.

I will sit enthroned.

I will ascend above the clouds.

I will make myself like the Most High.

Now compare that to:

Crowley: "Do what thou wilt."

The 60s and 70s: "If it feels good, do it."

The sexual revolution: "My body, my rules."

Modern identity ideology: "I define myself."

That is not cultural drift.

That is Lucifer's sermon evolving through technology.

And Revelation 13 is where that sermon graduates into mandatory worship.

Jezebel appears in Revelation Chapter 2. The Beast appears in Revelation Chapter 13. Even Aleister Crowley famously referred to himself as the Beast.

If you can't see the patterns by now... then yes—I might need another hobby.

Jezebel always follows the same path in Scripture:

Seduction first.

Control later.

Spiritual Death last.

She trains people to love themselves, to redefine morality, and to confuse devotion with desire. By the time Revelation 13 arrives, the world has already been fully discipled into "my way."

And if you're unfamiliar with the characters in this final act, here's the nutshell version:

Satan is a master counterfeiter.

God reveals Himself as:
Father
Son
Holy Spirit

Satan presents his own counterfeit trinity:
The Dragon — counterfeit father
The Beast — counterfeit christ
The False Prophet — counterfeit spirit

| 279

A counterfeit kingdom.

A counterfeit gospel.

A counterfeit salvation.

So when the Beast finally says, "Worship me or starve," the world responds, "As long as I can still choose me."

In other words, "worship me or starve" means that survival becomes tied to allegiance. Don't take my word for it — in Revelation 13:16–17 it says: "He causes all, both small and great, rich and poor, free and slave, to receive a mark on their right hand or on their forehead, and that no one may buy or sell except one who has the mark." Really take that in for a second... Aren't we starting to see the birth pains of that happening? A one-world, global commerce and banking system. AI transforming industry. Even on the top Christian music charts, AI personalities—not humans, but algorithms—are now producing songs that sound catchy and worshipful, but without the Holy Spirit breathing through a human vessel. And Christians are eating it up online, replaying the music, and pushing it to the top of the charts, often without realizing the subtle shift happening under their feet.

Every global tyrant in scripture rises through controlled provision. Which means the final war is not fought over theology first. It's fought over who feeds you. That's why the dinner table is the answer. Not the throne room.

13 = Nimrod—thirteen generations after Adam—stood in Babylon and declared, "Let us make a name for ourselves."

Do you see the pattern?

Collective human pride.
Centralized power.
Controlled unity.
God replaced by system.
Revelation 13 is Babylon perfected.

Not with bricks.
With bandwidth.

Not with towers.
With artificial intelligence and technology.

Not with one king.
With one global ideology.

This book has tracked the pattern:
Eden = choice
Babylon = system
Sinatra = soundtrack

The sexual revolution = the body
Jezebel = seduction
Revelation 13 = enforcement

That is not chaotic.
That is terrifyingly ordered.
In Revelation 13, the wolf no longer hides in sheep's clothing.

The choice becomes stark.

Choose who you worship.

Many will believe they are choosing freedom.
But they will actually be choosing permission to survive without their Creator—the Lover of their soul.
Revelation 13 is the last place in the Bible where:
Choice still exists.
Neutrality still pretends to live.
Compromise still feels survivable.

Revelation 13 is the last human crossroads.
Which means this ending is not literary.
It is prophetic architecture.
And what this investigation ultimately reveals is this:

Choose this day.

If this book has led you through questions of power, seduction, culture, celebrity, trauma, rebellion, spiritual authority, father wounds, Jezebel, Babylon, music, sex, fame, and fear—then Revelation 13 is | 281 where every one of those threads finally knots into a single moment of decision.
This is not a chapter about the future alone.
It is a mirror.

Revelation 13 reveals what happens when human choice becomes weaponized—when the spirit of "my way" no longer whispers through culture but stands at the center of the world demanding worship.
This is not myth.

This is not metaphor only.

This is the final form of rebellion.

The first beast rises from the sea—a final global political power empowered by hell itself. One of its heads is mortally wounded and then miraculously healed. The world marvels.

And then the chilling words echo through history:

"Who is like the beast? Who can make war with him?"—Revelation 13:4 (NKJV)

The False Prophet performs signs so spectacular that fire falls from heaven. He enforces worship. He animates an image. And then the system tightens:

No mark.

No buying.

No selling.

This is not folklore.

This is economic worship.

For the first time in human history:

Survival is tied to allegiance.

Commerce is conditioned on confession.

Eating is regulated by worship.

The world no longer merely tolerates the Beast.

It depends on him.

And then comes the number:

Man at the end of himself.

Seven is God's number.

Six is the number of man.

666 is humanity attempting divine status without God.

The final anthem of:

"I did it my way."

"I answer to no one."

"I define truth."

"I become my own god."

The mark is not only on the skin.

It is on the will.
On behavior.
On belief.
On identity.
On ownership.

This is my way versus Thy will—made visible.

Revelation 13 is one of the most revealing chapters in the Bible.
It removes illusion.
It strips away religious camouflage…
Cultural ambiguity…
Comfortable compromise…

You either worship the Lamb aka Jesus Christ.

Or you worship the system.
There is no middle lane.
There is no private neutrality.
The Beast never begins with terror.

He starts with:
Security
Unity.
Prosperity.
Stability.
Peace.

But the price is conscience.

And once conscience is traded, chains are no longer needed.

Revelation 13 does not end with heaven or hell.

It ends with calculation.
Think.
Discern.
Choose.

Because when the end truly comes, the final sin will not be ignorance.

It will be preference.

Revelation 13 is not about microchips first.
It is about ownership of the will.

Who defines truth.
Who defines worship.
Who defines survival.

It reveals where a lifetime of saying "my way" truly leads.

The Silver Lining

Revelation 13 is a warning. It's an opportunity.

The Very Fact That God Warns Means Rescue Is the Goal

Think about this for a moment:
If God's only intention was judgment,
He would not have written Revelation at all.

Revelation exists because:

• God still invites

• God still warns

• God still rescues

• God still marks His own before the world marks anyone else

Revelation 13 only exists because Revelation 7 already happened.
Before the mark of the beast ever appears,

God seals His people first.
Hell always imitates late.
Heaven always moves first.
That's the silver lining.
And when it's all said and done…
when the systems fall,
when the Beast is silenced,
when the dust of human rebellion finally settles,

the last image Scripture gives us is not fire in the sky—

It's a table.

Which feels almost absurd, considering how violent the story becomes. Kings rise and fall. Empires crush. Deception floods the earth. Revelation 13 thunders with economic control, forced allegiance, global pressure, survival by compliance. The darkest hour in human history. The loudest moment of evil's reign.

And then—almost offensively gentle—the camera pans.

Not to another battlefield.
Not to another throne.
But to candlelight.

Because it is no accident that when the end of the world arrives, the story takes us back to a dinner table.

We've seen this table before.

We saw it when David wrote, "You prepare a table for me in the presence of my enemies." Not a bunker. Not an escape tunnel. A table. While the threat still breathes. While the war is still close. God does not just defeat fear—He humiliates it by feeding His children in front of it.

We saw the table again in an upper room where Jesus broke bread and said, "This is My body." On the very night betrayal was already in motion, heaven still chose a meal. The cross was coming. The whip was coming. The nails were coming. And Jesus still set a table.

And then—quietly, almost hidden inside the warnings of Revelation itself—we hear these words spoken not to the world, but to the lukewarm church:

"Behold, I stand at the door and knock. If anyone hears My Voice and opens the door, I will come in—and dine with him, and he with Me."

Not a threat.

Not a demand.

An invitation.

At the very moment when the Beast will one day force a mark, Jesus still chooses to knock.

At the very moment when survival will be traded for allegiance, Jesus still offers relationship without coercion.

At the very moment when the world is being taught that power is taken, Jesus reminds us that love must always be chosen.

And when history finally reaches its breaking point—when evil is exposed, judged, and removed—the Bible does not end with a funeral.

It ends with a wedding.

A wedding feast.

A celebration.

A long table stretched across eternity where nations are healed, wounds are mended, and the Lamb who was slain sits at the head—not as a tyrant, not as a conqueror drunk on power, but as a Bridegroom who kept His promise.

This has always been the silver lining hidden inside the storm.

Revelation is not a horror story about how the world ends.

It is a love story about how evil finally does.

The Beast rises fast.

But he falls faster.

Fear gets loud.

But love gets the final word.

And what looks like the collapse of everything is actually the restoration of what was always meant to be.

A family.

A table.

A Father.

Which means the true conflict of human history was never just about nations, systems, technology, money, or power.

It has always been about consent.

Hell has never needed permission.

It only uses pressure.

But heaven has always waited at a door.

Knocking.

One choice leads to survival.

The other leads to a seat at the table.

One choice leads to a system that always devours its own.

The other leads to a Kingdom where even death is swallowed whole.

And in the end of that battle between Good and evil—Heaven does not evacuate. Heaven descends. The New Jerusalem comes down out of the sky, not as a fortress, not as a kingdom of fear, but as a family table, a wedding feast, a city where every tear is wiped away and every scar redeemed. The last scene is not escape—it is invasion theology: God Himself moves into the heart of His creation.

And when the smoke clears, when evil is finished, when the war is over, you won't be standing alone before a throne hoping you chose correctly.

You'll be sitting.
Candlelight flickering.
Bread broken.
A cup lifted.

And across the table, the Creator of the universe—the same One who knocked, the same One who waited, the same One who bled—will look at you and say, at last:

"Welcome home."

FINAL REFLECTION

The Debate…

My sincere prayer and declaration is that this book changes your life the way it's changed mine. Whether you grew up Pentecostal like I did, Catholic, or you're someone still trying to make sense of it all—I pray these pages have stirred something deeper than religion.

Because at the end of the day, this isn't about where you worship or how.

It's about why.
And it's about Who.

Hopefully, this book has challenged you to look past denominations and traditions—to look beyond buildings and bulletins—and to look straight into the eyes of Truth Himself.

But since the conversation around the Church is still unfolding, let's address the ongoing debate.

The same breaking news story that opened this book is still echoing across the Church as these pages close.

Pope Leo XIV's *Mater Populi Fidelis*—"The Mother of the Faithful People of God"—had barely dried in ink before it set the world talking.

Some called it courage.

Others called it confusion.

But no one could deny what it did: it turned the world's attention, even if for a moment, back toward Jesus.

The decree, issued in the first week of November 2025, instructed Catholics to stop using the titles *"co-redeemer"* or *"co-redemptrix"* for Mary.

The Vatican explained that while her role in bringing the Savior into the world was sacred, it was still subordinate—because only Jesus saved humanity through His death on the cross.

Whatever the pope's intention, there's grace in what remains: even now, more than a billion souls have been pointed straight back to the cross.

Across sanctuaries and timelines, believers are still debating, defending, explaining.

But maybe this moment isn't about who's right—it's about who's real.

Because if even the oldest institution can change its language overnight, maybe Heaven is reminding us that only one Word never changes.

I tread carefully here, as I did in the chapter on The Spiritual Autopsy.

Because this isn't about rivalry; it's about revelation.

It's about realizing that God's heart was never locked behind stained glass or denominational walls.

Man-made traditions, no matter how noble, can be fallible.
Human voices can drift.
Councils can shift.
Opinions can harden into dogma, and dogma can calcify into walls that hide the face of God.

That's why Jesus warned the Pharisees about "teaching as doctrines the commandments of men" (Matthew 15:9 NKJV).

Every generation faces the same temptation—to trade encounter for ceremony, revelation for repetition.

So while the world debates decrees and doctrines, here's what still matters most:
Who do you trust:

When it counts?
When it's your family on the line.
When your future hangs by a thread.
When your heart is breaking and no institution can fix it.

That's when theology stops being theory.

That's when faith becomes personal.

That's when you find out whether your foundation is built on rock—or on sand that shifts when the headlines change.

If your faith is anchored in a system that separates you from direct access to God, that can be dangerous.
Spiritually dangerous.

So before this final page turns—before the noise rises again—I invite you to come back to the Source Himself. Let's end this book—in total surrender.

Because while men argue, heaven still whispers the same invitation.

A Prayer for Truth and Renewal

Join me.

Father God, I come before You—heart to heart—acknowledging that You are the Creator of the heavens and the earth.
I confess with my mouth that I believe You love me.
I believe You want a relationship with me.
I believe that Your Son, Jesus Christ, was crucified on that tree, beaten and murdered to pay for the sin and the evil of this world—including my own.
But I also believe He did not stay dead.
On the third day, through Your Holy Spirit, He came back to life.
I receive Jesus Christ as my Lord and Savior.

I don't know everything, but I know that I'm hungry for truth and purpose. I ask You, God—and Holy Spirit—to reveal the truth regarding my life.
I renounce any and all agreements I may have made, knowingly or unknowingly, with darkness.

Holy Spirit, fill me with Your presence so I may be a bold witness to my family, to my community, and to the world.
And Father, if there is anything in my life—including relationships or even religious teachings—that has blinded me, reveal it to me.

I now speak and declare the authority that Jesus Christ gave me.

I call in the shalom—the peace—of God into my heart, my home, and my surroundings.

Wherever I go, let Your goodness and mercy follow me.

Let the atmosphere shift when I walk into a room—not because of me, but because of Who lives inside me.

In the name above every name—Jesus Christ, my Lord and Savior, I pray.

Amen.

ABOUT THE AUTHOR

Thirteen years ago, Stevie Prince sat outside the Trinity Broadcasting Network campus—near its on-site Christian library—with nothing left but questions and a book in his hands. Just moments earlier, he'd been turned away at a Wendy's down the street, standing at the counter counting pocket change, a dollar short of a chicken sandwich. He had spent some of the last money he had on that book—a study on spiritual warfare—hoping to find answers.

In front of him sat a bottle of Strawberry Fanta, a pack of chocolate turtles, and a lake that felt like the only piece of peace left. His businesses had collapsed, his plans had unraveled, and life as he knew it had hit rock bottom.

That moment—captured in a photo now included in the gallery of this book—became the quiet genesis of something he never saw coming. What began as a few journal entries written to wrestle with

God slowly became a manuscript. Now, thirteen years later, those same pages have become *Where Was God?* The connection to the number thirteen—and what it reveals in Chapter 13—is nothing short of staggering.

Prince is an author, musician, and storyteller whose work blurs the line between mystery, theology, and modern culture. Known for his cinematic writing and fearless approach to difficult questions, he creates what he calls spiritual investigations—projects that blend the grit of real life with the awe of divine truth.

A son of pastors, Prince grew up inside the glass house of ministry, witnessing both the beauty and the brokenness behind the pulpit—an experience that shaped his voice with empathy, authenticity, and relentless curiosity about what he calls the paradox of faith.

Before writing *Where Was God?*, he had already built a diverse creative career—serving on the Grammy Awards Nomination Review Committee, producing music across genres, and launching successful ventures spanning real estate, media, and event production. But it was the quiet motel rooms, the heartbreaks, and the miracles that gave his art its heartbeat.

Prince is signed to WillHouse Media Group, a creative collective dedicated to books, music, and storytelling that awaken purpose and challenge the culture. Through his writing, podcasting, and film work, he continues to connect timeless truths with a generation hungry for meaning in a haunted world.

When he's not writing or recording, he can be found somewhere between Chicago and Nashville—surrounded by family, faith, and a notebook full of unfinished lyrics and new ideas.

Follow his journey:

www.SteviePrince.com

This photo was taken thirteen years ago. I spent my last few dollars on this book, asking myself the same questions you might be asking now: Where was God? Was God even real?

I didn't plan this moment. I didn't even realize this photo still existed until just a few weeks before this book went to print. And yet, after thirteen years of searching, questioning, and investigation, I've learned something sacred—God may not plan our pain or our mistakes, but He has a way of revealing that His fingerprints were always there... even when we couldn't see Him, working quietly behind the scenes, as any good Father would.

If we let Him, He can turn moments of pain into moments of celebration.

BIBLIOGRAPHY & PROOF

Where Was God?

Charlie Kirk — Premonitions & Text Messages
New York Post.

"Charlie Kirk Predicted His Own Assassination in Chilling Text Messages to Candace Owens." New York Post, November 1, 2025.

In the article, text messages attributed to Kirk include:

"If I tell you the true prophecy I know in my gut it's really sad… Anyway I am not sure if I will live to see the end of this revolution."

Abraham Lincoln, Spiritualism, and Premonitions
Melton, Prior. "A Readable Sketch: Spiritualism at the White House." Boston Gazette, April 23, 1863. Lincoln Financial Foundation Collection, Allen County Public Library, Fort Wayne, Indiana.

Lamon, Ward Hill. Recollections of Abraham Lincoln, 1847–1865.

Edited by Dorothy Lamont Balcom. Chicago: A.C. McClurg & Co., 1895. Lamon, Lincoln's bodyguard, recounted that the president shared a premonition of his own death just days before the assassination.

History Staff. "Did Abraham Lincoln Predict His Own Death?" History Channel, originally published October 31, 2012; updated May 28, 2025.

Princess Diana — The Mishcon Note & Premonitions
Royal Observer Staff.

"Princess Diana Predicted Her Fatal Car Crash in Chilling Letter Two Years Before Paris Accident." The Royal Observer, August 27, 2025.

The article reports that in a note known as the "Mishcon Note," Diana allegedly warned in 1995 that sources told her a car crash would be staged to "get rid of her."

Owens, Candace. Public Commentator Podcast. Revealed text messages from Charlie Kirk dated February 15, 2024, in which he stated:

"We should chat soon. Catholicism is looking better and better."

Kato, Brooke. "Princess Diana Predicted a Car Crash Two Years Before Her Death in a Mysterious Note." New York Post, August 17, 2022.

Hampson, Laura. "What Is the Mishcon Note? How Princess Diana 'Predicted' Her Paris Car Crash." The Independent, August 31, 2022.

Royal Observer Staff.

"Princess Diana Predicted Her Fatal Car Crash in a Chilling Letter Two Years Before It Happened." The Royal Observer, August 27, 2025.

White House — Paranormal Testimonies
Kotb, Hoda (Host). "Is the White House Haunted?" TODAY Show (NBC Television Interview), October 15, 2018. Guest: Jenna Bush.

Kommel, Alexandra. "Séances in the Red Room." White House Historical Association, April 24, 2019.

Malcolm, Andrew. "Is the White House Haunted? Michelle Obama Reported Strange Things." Los Angeles Times Blog, April 23, 2009.

Truman, Harry S. Personal Letters to Bess Truman Regarding

White House Experiences. Truman Presidential Library, 1946.

Von, Theo. This Past Weekend Podcast, Episode #588. Vice President J.D. Vance recounted staying overnight in the Lincoln Bedroom, describing the experience as "creepy."

Michael Jackson
Jacobshagen, Michael. Interview by Daphne Barak on Sunday Night (Australia). According to Jacobshagen, Jackson allegedly wrote 13 letters before his death stating:

"They are trying to murder me" and "I am scared about my life."

John Lennon — Premonitions
Mintz, Elliot. Longtime friend and confidant of John Lennon and Yoko Ono. According to Mintz, Lennon and Ono visited a prominent palm reader in Greece who warned Lennon he would be killed "on an island." Yoko Ono reportedly told Mintz:

"Nothing can be prevented if it's destined to happen."

Cheatsheet.

"John Lennon: 2 Different Psychics Made Accurate Predictions About His Death." Confirms that Lennon was warned about his death both via a Greek palm reading and a psychic letter, supporting reports that he was aware of his mortality in advance.

27-Club, Premonitions & Cultural Patterns
Talseth, Thomas. "27-Club: Stars Who Died at Age 27, From Jimi Hendrix to Amy Winehouse." TheWrap, February 20, 2020.

The Independent.

Jimi Hendrix reportedly sat for a tarot reading in Morocco, drew [301] the Death card, and told friends he would die young. According to the article, Hendrix said:

"I'm going to die before I'm 30."

Over his final year he counted down the months, and two days before his death he told a journalist friend,

"I'm almost gone," after missing a planned performance due to intoxication.

Myles Munroe
Clips of Myles Munroe (Legacy YouTube Channel).

Video clip in which Pastor Myles Munroe states:

"My plan is to die with her," referring to his wife.

Marilyn Monroe — Mortality Awareness
de Dienes, André. Photographer of Marilyn Monroe.

In later interviews, de Dienes recalled Monroe asking him not to release certain photos until after her death and telling him in a sad voice:

"I think I'm going to die before you."

Monroe, who suffered from chronic insomnia and depression, often sought out dramatic, shadowed locations for photo sessions, including dark alleys and isolated rooftops in Beverly Hills—reflecting a fascination with mortality and a preoccupation with her own fragility.

Ronald Reagan — Spiritual Warfare
Reagan, Ronald.

"Remarks at the Annual Convention of the National Association of Evangelicals."

Orlando, Florida, March 8, 1983.

Gurley, Phineas D. "Funeral Sermon for Willie Lincoln." In The Death and Funeral of Willie Lincoln. Abraham Lincoln Online. Accessed October of 2025. https://www.abrahamlincolnonline.org/lincoln/education/williedeath.htm

Instead of a static list of sources that freeze the story in time, this book links you to a living archive — updated with new findings, video commentary, original documents, and official records as the investigation continues.

If you want the receipts —

if you want the proof —

visit SteviePrince.com/Proof

There, you'll find the evidence behind every claim, timestamped links, and the newest developments that couldn't fit between these covers.

Study Guide

Note to Readers:
Feel free to complete this study guide on your own or in a group—whether online, with friends, or in a church setting. Opening up conversations and exploring different perspectives is an important part of your spiritual journey and growth.

Instructions for Use:
- Read each chapter carefully before attempting this study guide.
- Answer the questions in your own words.
- Use the reflection space at the end to summarize your key insights.
- Feel free to reference Scripture or your personal experiences.

STUDY GUIDE – CHAPTER 1
Why Does God Allow Evil? The Freedom Paradox

Questions:

Q1: *Where is the first time the word evil appears in the Bible?*

_____

Q2: *What is the connection between the verbs 'take' and 'eat' in Genesis and at the Last Supper? Why might God use the same verbs in both situations?*

_____

Q3: *Does God get surprised when humans fail? Did He get surprised in the Garden of Eden?*

_____

Q4: *What is the definition of a paradox in this context?*

_____

Q5: *Did God already accept the Cross before He planted the first tree?*

_____

Q6: *Did God want a family of AI robots?*

_____

Q7: *What does it mean for humans to have free will?*

_____

_____

Reflection:

What key points in this chapter have given you food for thought?

_____

_____

Study Guide – Chapter 2
The Shot Heard Around the World:
Reopening Heaven's Oldest Cold Case

Questions:

Q1: Have you ever had moments in your own life that made you wonder why God allows suffering? If yes, explain:

_____

_____

Q2: Have you ever had moments in life when you felt like there was an unseen battle happening within you or around you? If yes, explain:

_____

_____

Q3: Do you believe in divine protection, or do you think that God doesn't care about our safety?

_____

_____

Q4: Have you ever felt confused when others around you call tragedy "holy"?

_____

_____

Q5: Have you ever lost someone too soon, or watched someone fall, leaving you with more questions than answers?

_____

_____

Q6: Do you think that religious people have a tendency to confuse others when it comes to explaining away tragedy?

_____

_____

Q7: Do you think that everything that happens is random, or do you see a pattern or thread unfolding throughout history?

_____

_____ | 305

Reflection:
What key points in this chapter have given you food for thought?

_____

_____

STUDY GUIDE – CHAPTER 3
Premonition or Permission: A Witch in the White House

Questions:

Q1: *Have you verified the evidence yourself? That President Abraham Lincoln had a dream days before his death, and that the Lincolns were inviting mediums into the White House? (Check the bibliography page of this book.)*

_____

_____

Q2: *How do you feel knowing that the house built to lead a nation was flirting with the spirit it was meant to resist?*

_____

_____

Q3: *Have you ever dabbled in witchcraft, tarot, card reading, or even games that seemed innocent but could have opened you up to the paranormal?*

_____

_____

Q4: *Do you believe in the spiritual world, or do you think that what you see with your eyes is all there is?*

_____

_____

Q5: *Do you think the stories about creepy occurrences in the White House were exaggerations, or was there something deeper going on?*

_____

_____

Q6: *Do you believe in the power of thoughts and words? Could thinking about something long enough—intentionally or accidentally—align you with what you fear most? If yes, explain:*

_____

_____

Q7: *Have you ever felt a premonition or had a dream that caused concern or worry about how something might unfold in the future? If yes, explain:*

_____

_____

Reflection:
What key points in this chapter have given you food for thought?

_____

_____

STUDY GUIDE – CHAPTER 4
Words Create Worlds: The Case Against Your Mouth

Questions:

Q1: *Do you think words are important? If yes, explain why:*

_____

_____

Q2: *Do you believe that, subconsciously, the words spoken to us by others—and the stories we allow ourselves to believe about ourselves—ultimately influence who we become?*

_____

_____

Q3: *Do you believe that Heaven keeps "receipts," even of the words we swallow?*

_____

_____

Q4: *Like in the hallway experience described by the author, standing up to a bully—do you think there are moments in life worth stepping in to condemn or cancel, whether it be actions or words of others?*

_____

_____

Q5: *Reflect on the Bible verse in Isaiah: "No weapon formed against you shall prosper, and every tongue which rises against you in judgment you shall condemn." Often, we focus on the first part but forget the second. What do you think the Bible is asking us to do here?*

_____

_____

Q6: *What is a clue that God takes words seriously?*

_____

_____

Q7: *Whether you're a fan or a critic of any person referenced in this book, do you think the Church is called to speak life and declare God's Word into situations we see happening to others, or that we may face ourselves? If yes, explain:*

_____

Reflection:

What key points in this chapter have given you food for thought?

_____

_____

STUDY GUIDE – CHAPTER 5
Ghosts, Keys, & Grace: Where Grace Meets the War

Questions:

Q1: *Have you ever asked yourself whether God is real? If yes, please explain:*

_____

Q2: *Have you ever wondered if evil is real in the supernatural sense? If yes, please explain:*

_____

Q3: *Have you ever had an unexplainable or seemingly supernatural experience?*

_____

Q4: *Do you believe in angels and demons? If yes, what is your worldview on this topic?*

_____

Q5: *Like the author, have you ever encountered something you believed was evil, but felt that—because of your lifestyle—you did not have the authority to confront it?*

_____

Q6: *Do you believe there is an invisible war happening in culture, influencing everyone from pop icons and leaders to everyday people? If yes, please explain:*

_____

Q7: *Do you think the devil tries to convince you that you have no God-given authority over him? Why would he do that?*

_____

Reflection:
What key points in this chapter have given you food for thought?

_____

_____

STUDY GUIDE – CHAPTER 6
The Gates of Hell: The Story They Hijacked

Questions:

Q1: *Did you know there was a location in the ancient world known as the Gates of Hell, a.k.a. the Gates of Hades? What additional insights can you add about the geography or what Jesus and His disciples might have seen that day?*

_____

_____

Q2: *Do you think it's a coincidence that Jesus chose to demonstrate one of the biggest spiritual declarations in history at this precise location?*

_____

_____

Q3: *What was the key question Jesus asked His disciples, and why was Peter's answer so important?*

_____

_____

Q4: *The Greek word for "church" is ekklesia. What is the original meaning of this word? Why would Jesus use it in front of the Gates of Hell, and what does that mean for us today?*

_____

_____

Q5: *On that day, did Jesus intend to give authority to a single man or to an entire governing body? Was this authority meant for an institution, or for anyone who becomes a follower of Jesus Christ?*

_____

_____

Q6: *Do you think someone or something—such as man-made systems—may have tried to hijack this story? What might they gain by making everyday believers think they don't have spiritual authority?*

_____

_____

Q7: *Why do you think Jesus uses the word "gates" when describing the cosmic battle between good and evil—the same battle in which the Church would participate? Why not use a different word, considering a gate is a defensive structure meant to keep people out? How does this comparison help you understand the battle?*

_____

_____

Reflection:

What key points in this chapter have given you food for thought?

_____

Study Guide – Chapter 7
The Martyr We Missed: Was It a Cover-Up?

Questions:

Q1: *What does the word martyr truly mean? Is it someone tragically murdered, or a bold witness for Christ?*

Q2: *How have podcasts, media, and even faith leaders misidentified or misrepresented what this word means?*

Q3: *Do you think Heaven wants to intervene on earth? If yes, what clues does the Bible give about how Heaven sees martyrs, Christians who were murdered, tragedy, warfare, and everyday Christian living?*

Q4: *Why did Jesus weep in Luke 19:41?*

Q5: *Have you ever felt like you missed moments in your life, or moments where you thought God should have intervened but didn't? If yes, please explain:*

Q6: *Do you think the lives of any individuals mentioned in this book could have turned out differently if they had received support in deep prayer from the Church when they needed it most?*

Q7: *In this chapter, the author quotes Scripture: "But the Church..." showing that although James was killed, when Peter was arrested and about to be sentenced to death, the church earnestly prayed using the Greek word extenos (to stretch out or reach beyond normal strength). Do you think the early Church always got everything perfect, or does the Bible give a raw, unedited account of believers still learning to exercise their authority?*

Reflection:
What key points in this chapter have given you food for thought?

STUDY GUIDE – CHAPTER 8
Spiritual Autopsy: The Jezebel and Balaam Connection
Questions:

Q1: *Who were Jezebel and Balaam in biblical times? What were they each known for?*

Q2: *Do you think it's a coincidence that a magazine named Jezebel in 2025 was associated with witchcraft or attempts to curse people of faith? Or do you see a connection, millennia later, of the same invisible force at work? If yes, explain:*

Q3: *Do you think there is tension between Catholic and Protestant beliefs regarding spiritual warfare and steps to take if you feel targeted by evil or curses? Or are the differences minor in the bigger picture?*

Q4: *Does the Bible only speak about Jezebel and Balaam in the Old Testament, or are they referenced in the New Testament as well? If yes, in what context?*

Q5: *What is idolatry? What is syncretism? When Scripture says God is a jealous God, is He insecure? Explain:*

Q6: *Have you ever, consciously or unconsciously, put your trust or worship into the creation instead of the Creator? Perhaps through organizations that added unnecessary barriers between you and God? Explain your experience:*

Q7: *In the book of Revelation, the church that Jesus rebukes—what does the name of that church mean in the original language, and why does it matter?*

Bonus Questions:
A: *Does the Bible anywhere state that believers have authority over all the power of the enemy?*

B: *Regardless of belief, fan status, or denominational alignment—if the Church is too busy focusing on trivial matters, while online publications boast about hiring witches and casting curses—have we begun to see the signs of a lukewarm Church?*

Reflection:
What key points in this chapter have given you food for thought?

Study Guide – Chapter 9
God Knew… But Did He Want It? The Devil's Alibi

Questions:

Q1: *What did Abraham and Mary Todd Lincoln's pastor do or say that may have influenced Mary Todd Lincoln toward spiritualism? If you were in her position, do you think you might have struggled to believe that God was a loving Father who wanted good for you? Explain:*

_____

Q2: *What does the Bible say about séances and necromancy? Please explain your understanding of this topic:*

_____

Q3: *Have you ever felt like someone you loved—or someone responsible for protecting you—either failed you or, worse, seemed to plan your pain? If yes, please explain:*

_____

Q4: *Have you ever felt that religion, or even your own thoughts, made God appear to be the orchestrator of your most painful moments? If yes, please explain:*

_____

Q5: *Why doesn't God step in and stop all suffering and tragedy? Why doesn't He force humans to follow His will?*

_____

Q6: *If God knows everything, yet practices what some call divine restraint, why does He require human cooperation to accomplish certain things? Do you believe human agency matters—or do you believe tragedy is part of a predetermined divine plan for a greater good? Explain:*

_____

Q7: *Can evil forces oppose God's will? What is the difference between a worldview that sees God as the divine architect behind all tragedy and suffering, versus a warfare worldview—where Jesus rebukes chaos, treats sickness as an intruder, and confronts oppression as an enemy rather than an instrument? Which worldview do you hold, and how do you biblically support your belief?*

_____

Reflection:
What key points in this chapter have given you food for thought?

_____

STUDY GUIDE – CHAPTER 10
The Inheritance Clause: You've Been Served

Questions:

Q1: *In your own words, define what an estate plan is and what purpose it serves:*

_____

_____

Q2: *What is a Last Will and Testament, and how does it function within the context of inheritance and legal authority?*

_____

Q3: *In general terms, what does it mean to inherit something? How does inheritance differ from earning or being given a gift?*

_____

Q4: *Imagine you legally inherited a house. When you arrive to take possession, you discover squatters living inside. How would you respond, and what legal rights would you assume you have in that situation?*

_____

Q5: *List at least five Bible verses where you see legal, covenantal, or inheritance-based language that mirrors concepts such as estate law, wills, or testament:*

_____

Q6: *When you pray, what has your spiritual posture most often resembled— bold and confident like a son or daughter who understands their inheritance, or hesitant like a servant asking for something you are not certain belongs to you? Please explain your answer:*

_____

_____ |313

Q7: *What key truths, challenges, or revelations from this chapter stood out to you the most, and why?*

_____

_____

Reflection:

What key truths, challenges, or revelations from this chapter stood out to you the most, and why?

_____

STUDY GUIDE – CHAPTER 11
Baptized in Fear: A Haunted Generation

Questions:

Q1: *What does it mean to be haunted by something—emotionally, psychologically, or spiritually? How would you personally define being "haunted"?*

_____

Q2: *Have you ever experienced trouble sleeping, recurring nightmares, night terrors, or sleep paralysis? If you feel comfortable, briefly describe your experience and how it affected you:*

_____

Q3: *Why do you think modern pop culture—through movies, music, and media—promotes fear so intensely? Do you believe there is something deeper or spiritual behind this emphasis on fear? Please explain your perspective:*

_____

Q4: *Do you believe sleep paralysis can be explained purely through medical or neurological causes? Do you think it may have a spiritual dimension? Or could it be a mixture of both? Explain your view:*

_____

Q5: *On which day of creation did God rest, according to Genesis?*

_____

Q6: *Why do you think spiritual rest is so important to God? What do you believe happens to a person—mentally, emotionally, and spiritually—when true rest is missing from their life?*

_____

Q7: *Regarding individuals like Lincoln and others mentioned in this chapter and throughout the book: Who do you believe was behind their fear, their dreams, and their premonitions? Do you see these as warnings from God, or as something darker attempting to shape their beliefs through deception and fear? Explain your reasoning:*

_____

Reflection:
What key truths, questions, or personal realizations did this chapter stir in you about fear, rest, or spiritual influence?

_____

Study Guide

STUDY GUIDE – CHAPTER 12
The God Who Throws Parties: Scandal at the Tree

Questions:

Q1: *Have you ever experienced bullying, whether as the one being targeted or as someone who participated in bullying? If you feel comfortable sharing, what did you learn from that experience?*

_____

_____

Q2: *Imagine someone you love—perhaps a child in elementary school—is being bullied on a playground next to a tree. If you could, would you shrink yourself to their size and step into that playground to provide support? How does this example, in comparison to God shrinking Himself to human size and entering the world, help you understand the heart of our Father?*

_____

_____

Q3: *What does it mean to you personally to know that God prepares a table for you in the presence of your enemies? How does this truth change your perspective on adversity?*

_____

_____

Q4: *How have you traditionally viewed God—as a serious God in heaven, keeping score of your failures, or as a Father who throws parties for His children? Please explain your viewpoint or personal experience:*

_____

_____

Q5: *Where did Jesus perform His first miracle—at a funeral, in a church, or at a wedding feast (i.e., a party)? What does this setting reveal about the heart of God?*

_____

_____

Q6: *Do you see a recurring pattern in Scripture where heaven celebrates redemption, or where someone or something lost is found? If so, please explain:*

_____ |315

_____

Q7: *In your own life, what are some moments where God has taken situations that could have been painful and turned them into blessings or celebrations of His faithfulness?*

_____

_____

Reflection:

What key insights, personal revelations, or challenges from this chapter stood out to you most? How can you apply these lessons to your life?

_____

STUDY GUIDE – CHAPTER 13
The People's Choice: My Way

Questions:

Q1: *Have you ever noticed or reflected on the superstition surrounding Friday the 13th? Please share any thoughts, beliefs, or experiences you have had regarding superstition or perceived bad luck:*

Q2: *According to Scripture or biblical accounts, how many times did Satan, also called Lucifer, use the words "I will" before being cast out of heaven?*

Q3: *If God grants humans true free will, can humans—or even spiritual beings—choose to oppose God's will and act according to their own desires? How does this understanding shape your perspective on freedom and human responsibility?*

Q4: *Why do you think individuals like Aleister Crowley, and other people influenced by evil, placed such strong emphasis on human will and personal choice? What lessons can be drawn from this focus?*

Q5: *How is the number 13 connected to rebellion, witchcraft, or spiritual opposition? Please explain your understanding:*

Q6: *In Hebrew tradition, what significance or meaning does the number 13 carry? How might this relate to rebellion or divine law?*

Q7: *What does Galatians 3:13 teach us about redemption and the curse of the law? What does this verse mean to you personally, and how does it influence your understanding of spiritual authority?*

Reflection:

What key insights, questions, or revelations did this chapter raise for you about human will, rebellion, and spiritual choice? How can you apply these lessons to your own life?

DIRECTOR'S CUT

God Is Love = 13

In Hebrew, the number 13 signifies love—ahavah—and oneness—echad. I never planned for that to be the thread tying this entire investigation together. I didn't outline it. I didn't map it. I didn't try to force it. It simply kept appearing—like a whisper behind the evidence board, as if Someone else had taken over the case file. And maybe "appearing" is the wrong word. It felt more like pursuing.

I never set out to write a book around a number. Thirteen years ago, the last thing I wanted was to be an author. I ran from ministry. I ran from God. I ran from myself. Yet the day I hit rock bottom—the same photo in the gallery—you can literally see me holding a book. Thirteen years later, I'm releasing my first one. You can call that coincidence. I tried to.

But then more breadcrumbs came.

The thesis of Chapter 13 centered around Sinatra's *My Way*—a prophetic picture of humanity choosing its will over God's. I never planned to tie Paul Anka into that chapter. He wasn't even on my radar. Then, at the very end of this manuscript, out of nowhere, HBO releases his documentary *His Way*. Same month. Same week. I turn on Jimmy Kimmel and see Paul Anka—suddenly back in the cultural spotlight—talking about the very song I'd been wrestling with for months. Coincidence, right?

I brushed it off. I stayed focused.

Until I looked into his life just a little deeper and learned something I had never known: he started his first vocal group at age 13. The man who wrote *My Way*—the cultural backbone of Chapter 13—began his musical story with the very number that kept showing up on my evidence board. Then I discovered he released his biography in 2013.

And that one of his hits, written for Buddy Holly, peaked at number 13 after Holly's death.

That's probably nothing, right?

I thought so too… until the day we finalized this manuscript.

I was driving home from dropping off my daughter, listening to a Turning Point USA podcast. Frank Turek—one of the last people in the car with Charlie—blurts out the number 13. I didn't know why it jolted me, but it did. I looked it up. Charlie started TPUSA 13 years before his assassination. And then I realized something that truly stopped me in my tracks:

I turned in this manuscript exactly 13 weeks after Charlie Kirk was murdered.

It was in that moment I realized this book was never about one man, one culture, or one era—it was a message from God to humanity.

None of that was planned. None of it curated. None of it manipulated. That's why, at first, these facts felt like afterthoughts—because that's how they came: late, unexpected, uninvited, but perfectly timed. Like Someone else wanted them on the page.

So I asked myself… is God trying to show me something?

I did something I had never done: I consulted with Hebrew rabbis. And what they shared didn't just add to the investigation—it completed it.

Because long before pop culture twisted the number 13 into | 319 superstition, God used it to reveal love.

After the catastrophe of the golden calf, when Israel broke the covenant and God's anger burned hot, Moses begged for mercy. And God responded by unveiling what Judaism considers one of the holiest revelations in Scripture: the 13 Attributes of Mercy. In Exodus 34:6–7, God proclaims thirteen descriptions of His character—thirteen ways He forgives, restores, heals, and holds His people close. For thousands of years, these attributes have formed the backbone of Jewish repentance prayers. God was saying, "This is who I am when you fail." Mercy first. Grace first. Covenant love stronger than covenant betrayal.

And Jericho? Same pattern.

In the book of Joshua, God tells Israel to march around the city once a day for six days and seven times on the seventh. That's $6 + 7 = 13$ total laps. The walls didn't fall on lap six or lap twelve—they fell on thirteen, the moment symbolizing God adding His power to human obedience. Thirteen became the picture of what happens when God steps into the story. The impossible falls.

And then came the detail that silenced me:

The chapter of the Bible known worldwide as "The Love Chapter" —the chapter read at weddings, whispered at hospital bedsides, quoted when the world needs hope—1 Corinthians 13.

Love is patient.

Love is kind.

Love never fails.

The greatest of these is love.

CHAPTER 13.

The very number Hebrew ties to love and oneness.

The number this investigation kept circling back to like a lighthouse in the fog.

Everywhere I turned, the same truth surfaced:

Thirteen is not the number of fear.

It is the number of love.

The number of mercy.

The number of "God is with us."

Isn't that what we celebrate on Christmas? Around a tree... Emmanuel, God with us. Who would ever think to connect that moment to the number 13?

After months of following the evidence, pulling threads,—walking through tragedy, cultural patterns, biblical texts, and modern events, I finally realized the message staring me in the face:

God loves us. All of us. Relentlessly.

Even when we don't feel Him. Even when circumstances look brutal. Even when our hearts break in ways that make no sense. He is behind the scenes, weaving redemption out of what He did not cause. He is the Father who refuses to waste pain. The Father who moves mountains quietly. The Father who steps into the dark with mercy, not punishment.

So at the end of this investigation—after all the data, theology, patterns, and revelations—I leave you with the simplest, most powerful four-letter word in the universe:

LOVE.

No matter what you've done.

No matter what you believe about yourself.

No matter what others have spoken over you.

God is relentless, unshakeable, unchanging love.

And His love—for you—equals 13.

"For God so loved the world that He gave His only begotten Son, that whoever believes in Him shall not perish but have everlasting life." | 321

— John 3:16 KJV

As we end this journey together, I want to remind you that everything in this book—every reference, every quote, every moment we examined—comes strictly from information that is publicly available. This investigation was never about judging the hearts or intentions of any person mentioned, but about exploring spiritual patterns, cultural moments, and the questions we all carry.

No individual, organization, or public figure referenced within these pages has participated in the creation of this book, nor have they reviewed, approved, contributed to, or endorsed any portion of its contents. Their appearances arise only from statements, interviews, and events already on the public record.

This work was written with humility and reverence, not to assign blame, but to seek understanding. If you would like more context on how this book was approached, please see the Author's Note at the beginning.

NOTES

www.ingramcontent.com/pod-product-compliance
Lightning Source LLC
Chambersburg PA
CBHW021215130626
46554CB00004B/1227